CESARE BECCARIA

and the Origins of Penal Reform

CESARE BECCARIA

and the Origins of Penal Reform

MARCELLO MAESTRO

Foreword by Norval Morris

Temple University Press

PHILADELPHIA

TEMPLE UNIVERSITY PRESS, Philadelphia 19122
© 1973 by Temple University. All rights reserved
Published 1973
Printed in the United States of America

International Standard Book Number: 0-87722-024-7
Library of Congress Catalog Card Number: 72-91133

CONTENTS

FOREWORD

THIS first full biography in English of Cesare Beccaria is particularly timely. We are at one of those turning points in the philosophy, sociology, and practice of criminal punishments when, as it has so often done since it was first published in 1764, Beccaria's *On Crimes and Punishments* again pushes itself into the forefront of scholarly consideration. It is both interesting and of assistance to understanding Beccaria's doctrine to have a sense of the pattern of his life.

Beccaria was, of course, one of the leading early opponents of capital punishment. The final vindication by the Supreme Court of his view of the social inutility of this punishment, and of its unconstitutionality, confirmed the quality of Beccaria's perceptive vision. But *On Crimes and Punishments* is of present importance for another reason: in it Beccaria outlined a philosophy of punishment, based on balanced *retributive* principles, which, in the view of many, not only has secure philosophic foundations but also offers our best contemporary guide to a humane and efficient criminal justice system.

Beccaria summarized his philosophy of punishment in these words: "In order for a punishment not to be an act of violence of one or of many against a private citizen, it ought to be public, prompt, necessary, the minimum possible in the given circumstances, proportionate to the crime, dictated by the laws." This is an admirable statement. If achieved it would banish brutality and revolt from our prisons and would bring order and decency to our criminal justice system. Its achievement would, of course, be no light task. It would involve major reorganization of our methods of recruiting, training, organizing, and deploying police; it would compel the courts to give meaning to the constitutional mandate of a speedy and public trial instead of relying on our present semi-secret dispositive processes of charge and plea bargaining; and it would bring a new day, an entirely new day, to corrections.

There are occasions when principle must break through practice, and such an occasion we now face in the criminal justice system of the United States. Years of rhetorical investment in law-and-order campaigns and in reforms at the level of tinkering and cosmetic changes have led to a criminal justice system which is racially discriminatory, pervaded by uncontrolled discretions, and which provides grossly inadequate community protection. Beccaria's writings have clear contemporary significance, and many thoughtful people working in the criminal justice system and studying it are coming to that realization.

Beccaria's influence on America is not new, but it is suddenly of larger promise than before. John Adams quoted Beccaria powerfully in 1770, when he exemplified all that is good in the role of the defense counsel by representing the British soldiers charged in the "Boston Massacre." Thomas Jefferson relied heavily on Beccaria. And Beccaria was one of the mainstreams of influence on the Quakers of Pennsylvania in their innovative movement at the end of the eighteenth century towards a more humane system of punishment. Beccaria opposed excessive brutality, but at the same time he took a properly modest view of the role of the criminal sanction in the task of perfecting man and society.

The criminal law is not a rational mechanism for making men virtuous; we would be fortunate if it could become a helpful mechanism for protecting citizens against personal violence, against major depredations to property, and from serious interferences with governmental processes. To rely on it for a host of morally uplifting purposes and for the prevention of a whole range of "victimless" crimes would have appeared to Beccaria as an endeavor of wild stupidity, as indeed it is. His writings on heresy and the law are directly applicable to the present moralistic overreach of criminal prohibitions.

There is at present sharp disagreement on the purposes of punishment, the functions of prison, and the proper role of the criminal law. Scholars and practitioners of corrections are alike uncertain as to the moral foundations of their work; in particular there is pervasive anxiety about imprisonment as a social mechanism, and increasingly doubts grow that criminals can be coerced to "cures."

Dr. Maestro's *Cesare Beccaria* helps us to reach back to strong, simple, and sensible first principles. Enrico Ferri and later writers built a Positivist school of criminology which mistakenly moved away from Beccaria's principles. And the Positivists had some of their ideas taken over and developed by those who thought it possible to use the criminal law as an instrument of social reform and social regeneration, to turn institutions for young offenders into "reformatories," to turn prisons into "training institutions"; in short, benevolently to coerce men to virtue, to vocational skill, and to social discipline. At last we are learning that it cannot be done, or at least that it cannot be done coercively. If we limit our punitive reactions to more modest objectives of humane self-protection, we are more likely to create both a more socially protective criminal justice system and one that does not, in the name of rehabilitation, inflict cruel and unnecessary suffering on our fellow men.

As this excellent biography reveals, Beccaria was astonished by the worldwide impact of his book, *On Crimes and Punishments.* His views were set deep in established writings; he did not see anything revolutionary in them. But they were expressed with clarity, logic, and unpretentious precision at a time when those qualities were precisely what was needed to bring change to an inefficient and brutal criminal justice system—at a time like our own. He was a clear voice speaking simply at the right moment.

This biography performs a valuable service for the causes of law reform, police reform, judicial reform, and correctional reform in this country. Let a few words of Maestro's, summing up Beccaria's contribution, make the point:

> Justice requires a right proportion between crimes and punishments, but the purpose of penalties is to prevent a criminal from doing more harm and to deter others from doing similar damage. Beccaria was convinced that man remains barbaric if he inflicts cruel punishments,

that he degrades himself by becoming a spy, that he becomes accustomed to bloodshed if he is exposed to it. Beccaria wanted a society of kind and civilized people and he believed that the abolition of cruel punishments, including the death penalty, would contribute to the formation of such a society. In this sense his approach was moral rather than juridical, so that Beccaria may be considered not so much a leading criminologist as a builder of a more civilized society and of a better and more pleasant world. . . . This ability to see everything in human terms makes Beccaria stand out above the other jurists and above the specialists, and it explains why he was able to inspire so many people and lead the nations of the world on the paths he advocated.

It is time we learned from Beccaria. This biography may help us to do so.

NORVAL MORRIS

Center for Studies in Criminal Justice
The University of Chicago

PREFACE

Today the name of Cesare Beccaria is hardly known in the English-speaking world, and yet he is the man who, more than any other, contributed to the reform of the medieval criminal law still in force in the eighteenth century. He acquired fame also for his writings on economics and other subjects, he foresaw future trends in numerous fields, and offered farsighted proposals for the solution of many problems.

I present here the first complete biography of Beccaria in the English language. In the past only partial studies of him have appeared in English, contained in books of wider scope or in the prefaces to the English editions of his treatise *On Crimes and Punishments*. The existing studies of Beccaria in Italian, valuable as some of them are, also stress only certain aspects of his activity. In writing this book I intended, instead, to give a fully rounded account of his life and work on the basis of all the documents now available.

It is my special hope that this book will revive the interest of English-speaking people in a man once famous on both sides of the Atlantic. This renewed interest would be justified by the fact that many of Beccaria's ideas are as fresh and timely today as they were two centuries ago.

Many passages from Beccaria's writings and excerpts from his letters and from those of other correspondents are presented here in English for the first time. For the quotations from Beccaria's treatise *On Crimes and Punishments* I have availed myself of the existing translations by Farrer (London, 1880), Paolucci (Indianapolis, 1963), and by Kenelm Foster and Jane Grigson (London, 1964). My own translations of passages from other writings of Beccaria are based upon the Italian text of his works edited by Sergio Romagnoli (Florence, 1958). For quotations of other authors I have used the editions mentioned in the bibliography.

I would like here to thank Professor Franco Venturi of the University of Turin for his friendly interest in my work. I am also grateful to Professor Mario Romani of the Catholic University of Milan for keeping me informed of his most recent research on the still unpublished reports and notes of Beccaria and for supplying details and photostats of these documents. Finally, I want to thank Professor Irene Mahoney of the College of New Rochelle for her expert help in the revision of the manuscript.

M.M.

New Rochelle, N.Y.
Fall 1972

CESARE BECCARIA

and the Origins of Penal Reform

1

A Field in Need of Reform

IN 1764 a small book entitled *Dei delitti e delle pene* was published in Italy. It aroused such interest that two more Italian editions appeared within a short time, and translations in several languages were soon published in other countries. The author of the book, Cesare Beccaria, barely known until then, suddenly became famous throughout Europe and across the ocean.

Beccaria's book dealt with the state of criminal law. His opposition to arbitrary rule, to cruelty and intolerance, and his belief that no man had the right to take away the life of another human being constituted the moral basis on which his principles were built. His ideas not only had an impact on all the cultivated people of Europe and America, but influenced the attitudes of statesmen and governments, and brought about needed reforms.

In his lifetime Beccaria was greatly honored and admired: his cooperation was sought by Catherine the Great of Russia and Maria Theresa of Austria, and his writings were read and quoted by illustrious men of the time, from Voltaire to Thomas Jefferson, from Blackstone to John Adams. Why, then, in later years—especially in the English-speaking countries where he had had so many followers—

3

did Beccaria gradually lose his popularity? At the beginning of the twentieth century an English historian gave the following explanation: "Paradoxical as it may seem, the fame of a pioneer often becomes dimmer the more his efforts have been crowned with success."[1] Perhaps it is so, and a man writing early in the twentieth century might have thought that Beccaria's efforts had indeed been crowned with success—or at least that mankind was moving toward the realization of his ideals. Today, however, as we approach the end of this century, we know that the reality is different and that the civilized and gentle society for which Beccaria worked is not yet here. It seems right, then, still to consider him a pioneer whose fame should not become dimmer.

Milan in the Eighteenth Century

In 1764 few people expected an important book to come out of Italy, a country where the atmosphere was still heavy with the recollection of Giordano Bruno's burning at the stake and the trials of Galilei and Campanella. But a change for the better had taken place at the beginning of the eighteenth century, when Spain relinquished her control of Italy and was replaced by Austria as the dominant power in most of the country. Although Paris for some time had been the great intellectual center of continental Europe, signs of an Italian literary revival could be seen in the scholarly works of Vico and Muratori, and in the plays and essays of Goldoni, Baretti, and of Carlo and Gasparo Gozzi.

One of the Italian regions to become part of the Austrian dominions was Lombardy, with its capital city of Milan. It was then governed by Count Firmian, an enlightened representative of the empress Maria Theresa. Under his administration important public works were undertaken and beneficial reforms encouraged.[2]

The city of Milan, which has had many ups and downs in its long

---

1. Coleman Phillipson, *Three Criminal Law Reformers: Beccaria, Bentham, Romilly,* p. 100. Phillipson's book, although published in 1923, had been completed in 1914.

2. To be exact, not the whole of Lombardy came under Austrian rule at the beginning of the eighteenth century; the districts of Bergamo and Brescia remained under the jurisdiction of the Venetian republic.

Count Carlo Firmian was appointed minister plenipotentiary for Lombardy in 1758. He was entrusted with the civilian administration of Lombardy under Archduke Ferdinand of Austria (who was the titular governor and also had charge of military matters). Count Firmian, born in Trento in 1716, a friend of history, was then in a rising phase after a tragic seventeenth century when famine and the plague had wiped out two-thirds of its previous population. By the middle of the eighteenth century Milan had regained an important position among the cities of northern Italy. Its population of 120,000 was still much smaller than that of other European cities, but according to the chronicles of that period Milan was again lively and full of confidence in its future. In the center of the city, on the Piazza del Duomo, stood the imposing Gothic cathedral whose numerous spires at that time reached heights unmatched by any building in sight. The many new constructions visible inside and outside the city limits were a clear sign of faith in further expansion.

The ease with which Milan has always been able to rise again from its worst catastrophes is explained by its central position in the fertile Po valley, by its being ideally situated as the intermediary between Italy and the countries to the north, and by the energy and tenacity of the Milanese, who throughout history seem never to have been discouraged by unfavorable events.

Beccaria's Early Activities

In the eighteenth century Milan, of all Italian cities, had perhaps the closest contacts with the new humanistic currents of England and France. A Milanese élite of young intellectuals followed with great interest the literary and philosophical developments which were taking place across the Alps. Among these young intellectuals was the man who would soon become famous: Cesare Beccaria. Born in Milan on March 15, 1738, he was the first son of aristocratic though not very wealthy parents, Giovanni Saverio and Maria Beccaria. His full name and title were Marchese Cesare Beccaria Bonesana. With his two younger brothers, Francesco and Annibale, and his sister, Maddalena, he was brought up in the old family house on Via Brera.[3]

The Beccarias, like all the aristocratic families in Milan, were

---

writers and scholars, assembled during his lifetime one of the largest private collections of books and art works in Italy. He held his government position in Milan until his death in 1782.

3. According to documents in possession of the present owners, the property on Via Brera was acquired by the Beccaria family in the seventeenth century. The house, now 6 Via Brera, was renovated in the nineteenth century by Beccaria's son, Giulio, and changed hands several times after the extinction of the Beccaria family. At present, near the entrance door there is an inscription saying: "In this house Cesare Beccaria was born in 1738 and died on November 28, 1794."

Roman Catholics, and at the age of eight Cesare was sent to Parma to study in a private school directed by the Jesuits. Later in his life he was to complain that in that school he had received a fanatical education which had stifled the development of human feelings in his soul. This description, contained in a letter of 1766 to his French translator André Morellet, was certainly extreme. In any case, his years in Parma gave him a good cultural basis for his intellectual evolution. Early in his schooling he was noted for his sharp grasp of mathematics. The other children were so impressed by his talent that they called him *"Newtoncino"* ("little Newton"). His teachers found in him a vivid and fertile imagination, and also a tendency to change his mood between depression and excitement for the slightest reason.[4]

After studying for eight years in Parma Cesare entered the University of Pavia, where he studied law and received his doctor's degree on September 13, 1758, at the age of twenty. On returning to Milan he joined the *Accademia dei Trasformati,* a literary club frequented by many young men of the best Milanese society. Academies of this type, which flourished in Italy in the seventeenth and eighteenth centuries, had witty or ludicrous names, such as the Lunatics, the Extravagant, the Drowsy, the Apathetic, the Anxious, the Confused, the Fantastic, the Ethereal. In Milan the fashionable academy in those years was that of the Transformed, and there Beccaria met a number of writers and intellectuals, among them the poet Giuseppe Parini who later, in his satire *Il Giorno,* would castigate those Italian aristocrats who, interested only in their own well-being, led idle and meaningless lives.

Beccaria's debut at the academy was not much different from that of other new members. He wrote some poems in which he dealt in a light vein with various contemporary events and situations, and despite his timidity he read these poems at the academy meetings. No one would have predicted at that time that one of the most influential books of the century would soon be written by the author of those verses. At any rate, this type of literary exercise did not last long, for in 1760 Beccaria, then twenty-two, suddenly fell in love with a young girl of sixteen whom he had just met. She was the pretty and vivacious Teresa Blasco, the daughter of an army colonel. It was a storm

---

4. See Vianello, *La vita e l'opera di Cesare Beccaria, con scritti e documenti inediti,* p. 11.

in the life of the young man. Cesare and Teresa decided to get married immediately, but Beccaria's father was dead set against the girl and against a marriage which he thought was unwise. His threats did not prevent Cesare from seeing Teresa and from writing her the most passionate letters, like the following, written in the fall of 1760:

My dear spouse:

Let me call you by this sweet name which shall be my consolation through my whole life if you will remain faithful to me and if I will be able to earn your love.

I swear that when I will be your husband all my time will be spent in serving you, pleasing you, loving you, and doing everything that will make you happy and merry. . . .

You don't know, my love, how I suffer. I try not to show it, but I see my father and my uncle talking in secret and plotting something against you and me. Whatever they do, I am determined to marry you. . . .

My dear, have faith in me. Even if I should be jailed—it may well happen—I will never change. But I am afraid that if you or your parents hear that I may be thrown out of my house with the smallest allowance you will not stay by me, and this gives me a terrible anxiety. Please answer me on this point because I am ready to be miserable and homeless. I swear to God that I am ready to die rather than leave you.

Upset by his family's continuous opposition, Beccaria went to see Teresa's father to tell him of his difficulties with his own parents and of his fear that the marriage might result in his disinheritance and the breaking of his family ties. Teresa's father, with the confidence of a good army man, assured Cesare that he would intervene with his parents and in one way or another make them more amenable to the young people's desires.

But Beccaria's father would not be moved by either his son's insistence or by the colonel's threats, and Cesare, profoundly discouraged, yielded for a moment to his father's pressure. He wrote Teresa that after long reflection he had come to the conclusion that a marriage against his father's will would not be a happy one, and asked her to release him from his promises.

This was only a temporary weakness, however, and Beccaria soon regretted it. On February 14, 1761, he made his final decision and wrote the following letter, delivered promptly by hand:

My dear father:

I don't want to leave any doubt about my true and final decision. This is why I am stating it in writing, asking your forgiveness for what I am going to tell you in all sincerity.

Please be assured that only death can destroy my resolution, and the idea of death doesn't frighten me. I swear before God that I will not change my decision. I ask you in the name of Jesus Christ to stop putting obstacles to this marriage and to stop doing violence to my will and my conscience. Please leave me free to follow my destiny. If the result of my decision will be bad, as you say, it will be my fault, not the fault of my parents. I did everything I could in order to please you, against my own soul, but now I cannot change any more. I am ready to leave your house and to accept whatever little subsidy you will give me, but I ask you to let me do what I want. Otherwise I don't know what will happen to your poor son who has suffered all possible torments. I kiss your hand and ask for your fatherly blessing.

No fatherly blessing came forth, and Cesare's mother was just as obdurate. The marriage took place and the young couple had to start a life of poverty. It took more than a year before father and son made peace—a peace achieved through the intervention of Cesare's new friend, Count Pietro Verri. Knowing that nothing could be accomplished by reasonable discussion, Verri staged a melodramatic scene that produced the desired result. One day at dinner time the young couple were walking, as if by pure chance, in front of the family house on Via Brera, and Cesare asked if they might come in for a moment because Teresa had just had a fainting spell. In the house all rushed around Teresa who affected a slow recovery and showed with her tears that she was touched by so much care. It ended, as Verri had foreseen, with Cesare and Teresa obtaining his parents' forgiveness and being allowed to establish themselves in the family home.[5]

Friendship with Pietro Verri

Cesare had met Pietro Verri, ten years his elder, at the Accademia dei Trasformati. He was a cultured and ambitious man, with many intel-

---

5. For the full text of Beccaria's letters in the original Italian see Beccaria, *Opere,* ed. Romagnoli, vol. 2, pp. 829 ff. For the description of the reconciliation between Beccaria and his parents see pp. 930–32.

The uncle mentioned in one of Beccaria's letters to Teresa was his father's brother, Niccolò Beccaria, a cleric living at that time in the same house.

lectual interests, who was soon to make a name for himself as a writer and an economist. Having just returned to Milan from a long sojourn at the imperial court of Vienna, he discovered that the poet Giuseppe Parini was now the most admired member of the Trasformati. Finding it difficult not to be himself the star of the group, and wishing to have a small circle of his own, he decided to form in his home a rival literary club which he called *Accademia dei Pugni,* or Academy of Fists. Judging from this designation, it seems that Pietro Verri expected heated discussions in his club, although not necessarily the fistfights that the name implied.

Beccaria followed Pietro Verri to the new club, as did Pietro's twenty-year-old brother Alessandro, as well as several other friends of Pietro, such as Count Biffi, Alfonso Longo, Luigi Lambertenghi, the mathematician Paolo Frisi, and the economist Gian Rinaldo Carli.[6]

All the members of the group were young, serious, and full of goodwill. Every evening they read and discussed such authors as Shakespeare, Hume, Pope, Swift, Montaigne, Rousseau, Montesquieu, and Voltaire. In the Biffi collection of the Cremona library one can still see the notes written by these young scholars on the books that interested them. Beccaria was happy in this congenial society and had the greatest admiration for Pietro Verri, who for his part was quite impressed by Beccaria's talents, as can be seen from a letter written on April 6, 1762:

> Among the gifted young men who are forming a distinguished company at my home I will name a certain Marquis Beccaria, of good family . . . whose vivid imagination together with his careful

---

6. While Pietro Verri (1728–97) remained active in the literary and economic life of Milan, his brother Alessandro (1741–1816) later moved to Rome and wrote books on historical subjects, among them the once popular *Roman Nights.*
Paolo Frisi (1728–84) acquired a wide reputation in the scientific field; he wrote numerous essays on mathematics, physics, architecture, and cosmography. Alfonso Longo (1738–1804) became known for his contributions in the fields of economics and public law. Count Giovan Battista Biffi (1736–1807) stayed in Milan only a few years and then settled in his native Cremona; he was a bibliophile who had a predilection for the English language and literature. Luigi Lambertenghi (1739–1813) became active in the political field. Count Gian Rinaldo Carli (1720–95), the oldest in the group, was only an occasional participant in its activities; born in Capodistria (then part of the Venetian republic), Carli wrote widely on economics and other subjects, and in 1765 became president of the Supreme Economic Council of Milan. See Venturi, *Settecento riformatore—Da Muratori a Beccaria,* pp. 645 ff.

study of the human heart make of him an exceptionally remarkable man. . . . He is a profound mathematician, a good poet, with a mind apt to try new roads if he is not overcome by laziness and discouragement. He comes to see me every day, and after talking for a while, we study in silence in the same room.[7]

It is interesting to see that Pietro Verri had noticed the moody aspect in the character of Beccaria, whose lifelong activity, however, seems to belie the tendency toward laziness which Verri had mentioned.

The earnestness of these young men in their studies and discussions often did lead to the heated debates that Pietro Verri had anticipated. As we may see from a letter written some years later by Alfonso Longo to Pietro Verri, Beccaria often proved himself very stubborn in these discussions. Despite his admiration for Pietro, he did not always accept his friend's point of view and defended his own ideas with skill and tenacity. Fiery exchanges took place also between Beccaria and Alessandro Verri. Younger and less experienced, Alessandro would hold his own for a while, but in the end he usually gave in to Beccaria's insistent arguments. To be sure, these were intellectual discussions on literary or scientific matters, and even in their most vehement confrontations the debaters never lost sight of their idealistic motives.

This was an important period for Beccaria, who was then twenty-four. In July of 1762 his young wife gave birth to a little girl, Giulia, and at that time Beccaria published his first work: an essay on how to remedy the monetary disorder in Milan, entitled *Del disordine e de' rimedii delle monete nello stato di Milano nell'anno 1762*. He had chosen this monetary subject on the advice of Pietro Verri because it was arousing great interest among economists and financial experts. The fact that many different coins had free circulation in Milan had encouraged operations based on rates of exchange fixed arbitrarily by speculators. Several writers versed in monetary problems, among them Pompeo Neri and Gian Rinaldo Carli, had discussed the situation in various essays. They all had tried to find a remedy for the

---

7. Casati, *Lettere e scritti inediti di Pietro e Alessandro Verri*, vol. 1, pp. 153–54.

prevailing confusion, which was of great harm to the development of commercial transactions.[8]

Beccaria's contribution to the solution of the problem was a neat mathematical proposal based on the content of gold and silver in each coin, which he tabulated in his pamphlet. Having accepted the relation of fourteen and one-half to one in the values of gold and silver, and having ascertained the content of each in the different coins, Beccaria was able to calculate the rate of exchange of each coin against all the others. His principle was undoubtedly right, but his figures were incorrect because he had taken for granted that the grain, which was the unitary measure of the gold content, always had the same weight. Instead, the weight of the grain varied according to countries and mints. Despite this technical error, Beccaria's pamphlet aroused lively discussion and was taken into serious consideration by the state administration. In February 1763 some steps were taken in conformity with Beccaria's suggestions, and these first measures opened the way to the complete monetary reform enacted in 1777. Thus, Beccaria's essay turned out to be something more than an arithmetical exercise, and his name began to be known, at least in Milan.

Beccaria was not the only member of the Accademia dei Pugni who was busy writing in that period. Pietro Verri was then working on his *Essay on Happiness,* a philosophical study soon to be published in Leghorn. He had just finished an essay on methods to increase the commerce of Milan, which he later presented to the authorities and which earned for him an important place in the city economic council. As for Alessandro Verri, he was beginning to write a history of Italy, a work which, despite some merit, was in the end rather disappointing and was never published.[9]

By the beginning of 1763 Beccaria, having finished his first essay, was eager to do something else. Pietro Verri suggested a subject which "would be an excellent one for an eloquent and very imaginative man": a critical study of the existing criminal law.[10]

---

8. For an extensive survey of writings on monetary problems in Milan and other Italian regions around the middle of the eighteenth century see Venturi, pp. 443–522.

9. The manuscript of Alessandro Verri's history of Italy has been preserved by the descendants of the Verri family (see Venturi, pp. 715 ff.).

10. See Casati, vol. 1, pp. 189–90.

The idea appealed to Beccaria and in March 1763 he began to work on it. Although his degree in law from the University of Pavia provided him with a general background for his subject, there were many aspects which required investigation. Some information was supplied by Alessandro Verri, who had been named protector of prisoners, an honorary office which required him to visit persons in jail, listen to their grievances and needs, and intervene in their behalf when a pardon was considered possible. Beccaria, having gathered further information from other sources, was hard at work on his project in the summer of 1763 at his family country home in Gessate. At the end of July he wrote to a friend: "I will not be in Milan for another fifteen days, and I hope that by then my book on punishments will be well advanced."[11]

Back in the city, Beccaria continued his work. Every day he discussed his ideas with the Verris; at night he did his writing. Finally, in April 1764, the manuscript of Beccaria's treatise *On Crimes and Punishments* was ready; by then he had learned many things about the state of criminal law in the countries of the Western world.

Criminal Justice in the Eighteenth Century

Beccaria's keen mind enabled him to get to the essence of things. When he started his investigation on the conditions of the criminal system he perceived quickly what was fundamentally wrong with the existing laws. The main characteristics of justice as it was then carried out were confusion and cruelty. Contradictions and incongruities in the laws were due to the different influences that through the centuries had altered the old Roman code. Some of the old laws were still in existence, some had been changed, and some new ones had been added. The lack of rational codes and scales of punishments was the cause of unavoidable arbitrariness in the decisions of the judges. For certain crimes no penalty was specified and the judge was entitled to make his selection among the punishments provided for other crimes. Sometimes the penalty was specified, but the judge had the power to increase or diminish it considerably according to circumstances.[12]

---

11. See Beccaria, *Opere,* ed. Romagnoli, vol. 2, pp. 855–56.
12. For the state of criminal law in Europe in the eighteenth century see Maestro, *Voltaire and Beccaria as Reformers of Criminal Law,* pp. 1–13.

As for the characteristic of cruelty, it was considered dutiful—on the basis of a narrowly interpreted divine law—to apply literally the biblical "lex talionis" of an eye for an eye. Moreover, the supposed divine origin of this principle precluded any compromise or mitigation.

Superstition had long since entered the realm of justice, and the prosecution of witchcraft and sorcery had not yet ceased. It is true that the atrocities committed in connection with these imaginary crimes had decreased in number and had even disappeared in some countries, but in the English colonies of America the Salem trials had taken place as late as 1692, and in some European countries witches and sorcerers were still being tried and burned in the eighteenth century.

Suicide, under the influence of theology, was considered a crime. The possessions of the dead were often confiscated, and vengeance was wreaked on the corpse in the name of the law. In England, for example, people who committed suicide were buried at a crossroad after having stakes driven through their bodies.

A custom still in force in the eighteenth century was the right of asylum whereby fugitives from justice could find a sanctuary in churches and other sacred sites. This ecclesiastical privilege was responsible for the most absurd situations, such as the case of churches becoming not only places of shelter for criminals, but also repositories for large quantities of stolen goods. Not uncommon was the case of an outlaw who, in order to establish with absolute certainty his right to be sheltered, killed a passerby in front of a church and then rushed inside.[13]

The death penalty and bodily mutilations, rather than prison terms, were the usual punishments for the majority of crimes. For minor offenses the most frequent penalties were flogging and such corporal mutilations as slitting or piercing the tongue, and cutting or burning off the hand. For offenses such as perjury or bribery the customary penalty was the pillory; these devices were set up in public places, and the pains of exposure were increased by the jeers and insults of the onlookers. In Rome the pillories were erected on the Capitoline steps, and Cantù relates that the faces of the culprits were daubed with honey so they would attract flies.[14]

---

13. See Venturi, p. 33.
14. See Cantù, *Beccaria e il diritto penale,* pp. 18–19.

Capital punishments were of various kinds: burning at the stake was the regular punishment for heresy, while for other crimes the most usual forms of execution were hanging, quartering, and breaking on the wheel. In some cases the judges prescribed death penalties of a special kind. For example, when in 1757 an unbalanced man by the name of Damiens stabbed Louis XIV of France, the judges decided to inflict on the condemned man the most painful death they could devise. This gruesome story is told in Robert Anchel's book on crimes and penalties in the eighteenth century and in Voltaire's *History of the Paris Parliament*.[15]

At 7 A.M. on the day of his execution Damiens was led to the torture chamber for the purpose of extorting from him the names of accomplices—an impossible task, since it already had been established that he had acted on a personal impulse. In the torture chamber Damiens's legs were placed in devices called "boots," which could be squeezed gradually by means of wedges. After the insertion of eight wedges at intervals of fifteen minutes, every insertion being accompanied by horrible screams, the doctors who had been called to be present at the operation decided that it was not possible to continue "without the danger of an accident." The victim was then taken to the place of execution, in front of the Paris City Hall. The site was filled with all the Parisian rabble, wishing to enjoy the spectacle. French and Swiss guards kept order on all the surrounding avenues. The prisoner was placed on the scaffold and tied with ropes applied to his arms and legs. First, his hand was burned in a brazier filled with flaming sulphur. He was then pinched with red-hot tongs on his arms, his thighs, and his chest. On his open wounds molten lead and boiling oil were poured. This operation was repeated several times and every time the most terrible screams came from the wretched creature. After that, four big horses, whipped by four attendants, pulled the ropes rubbing against the inflamed and bleeding wounds of the patient. The pulling and shaking lasted a full hour. The arms and legs became more and more distended but remained attached to the body. The executioners then cut some of the tendons, and with some more pulling the limbs finally separated. Damiens, despite having lost

---

15. For the description of Damiens's execution see Robert Anchel, *Crimes et châtiments au XVIIIe siècle,* pp. 130–32, and Voltaire, *Oeuvres,* vol. 16, pp. 98–99; also Cantù, p. 16, where it is said that Damiens's innocent relatives were banished and his house demolished.

two legs and one arm, was still breathing and died only when the second arm was detached from his bloody torso. Arms, legs, and body were all thrown into a fire that had been prepared near the scaffold. It was evening by then; the judges, the high officials, the executioners, and all the spectators could now retire to their homes.

England and her American colonies were no exception as far as harsh punishments were concerned. In fact, in England and in the territories under English rule the death penalty was inflicted with incredible frequency for all kinds of crimes, even for very small thefts. Hanging was the regular form of execution, but a worse penalty was reserved for a man guilty of high treason: in accordance with an old custom he was dragged along the ground at the tail of a horse, with only a grate to protect his head from knocking on the stones; then he was hanged and from his still living body the entrails were pulled out and thrown in the fire; after that his head was cut off and the body quartered. In the eighteenth century this custom was somewhat softened: the entrails were pulled out *after* the condemned man had ceased to breathe.[16]

While punishments in England were just as cruel as elsewhere, the procedure there was much more advanced than in other countries. In fact, England had never adopted the inquisitorial procedure which had developed on the continent under the influence of the Roman church and the despotism of the rulers. The two main features of this procedure were the use of secret means in order to discover a culprit, and the employment of torture to obtain his confession. Torture was an elaborate institution: there was an *ordinary* and an *extraordinary* torture, according to intensity; the judge had full power to stop with the first or to go on to the latter. Torture was used to extort from the accused the confession of his crime (*preparatory* torture), and it was administered to persons already condemned in order to obtain from them the names of their accomplices (*preliminary* torture). All sorts of refined torments were described in the ordinances dealing with this subject.

England was the only European country which had resisted the inquisitorial system and had preserved an open procedure. Accusation

---

16. See Cantù, p. 17 (quoting from Blackstone); also Voltaire, *Oeuvres,* vol. 15, pp. 301–2.

was exercised freely by every citizen and the trials were confrontative, oral, and public. England had also developed the institution of the jury, an important step toward the organization of improved methods of justice. However, there were some weak points in the English system, one of them being that most of the laws were still unwritten and not easily accessible to the people.

The English procedure, however, also had its cruel sides. Trial by jury had to be expressly accepted by the accused, who had to declare that "he put himself upon the country." The accused who refused to pronounce these words and remained silent could not be tried. In order to make him talk one had recourse to the *peine forte et dure,* which consisted in stretching him on his back and placing over him an iron weight as heavy as he could bear. He was left that way until he died or spoke. A man would suffer these torments and lose his life in order to avoid trial and, therefore, conviction. In this way his lands and goods were not confiscated and were preserved for his family. This absurd proceeding was not abolished until the year 1772.

Such was the state of justice when in 1764 Beccaria wrote his treatise *On Crimes and Punishments.* Before Beccaria some enlightened men had already taken a stand against the worst aspects of the existing system, especially against the use of torture which seemed to many not only cruel but also absurd and misleading, since it often made people confess crimes of which they were innocent. Protests had also been directed against other objectionable practices, especially against the ease with which the death penalty was meted out for minor crimes.[17]

One of the first persons to take concrete steps toward a more humanitarian attitude in respect to criminal legislation was the founder and first governor of Pennsylvania, the Quaker William Penn, who in 1681 had received the charter from King Charles II that made him "master" of that province. Having the power to make laws and having faith in the people, Penn delegated to them more rights and privileges than the colonists possessed in any other American territory. He also engaged in the task of compiling a code of criminal laws more mild and rational than that of the mother country. Among

---

17. For a survey of humanitarian reactions against the state of criminal law before Beccaria see Maestro, pp. 14–50.

other provisions, Penn's code established that the death penalty should be inflicted only as a punishment for deliberate murder. This decision, however, was at such variance with the English laws of the time that the new code was considered dangerous and was annulled by Queen Anne, who had succeeded Charles II to the English throne. Although Penn's enlightened reform was temporary, its impact was a lasting one and it inspired a progressive attitude on the part of the lawmakers of Pennsylvania in later times.[18]

In the first part of the eighteenth century the protests against cruel punishments, torture, and other aspects of the criminal system became more numerous under the influence of the humanistic currents that had been developing in England and on the European continent. In Italy a first criticism of the existing conditions had come in 1742 from the historian Lodovico Antonio Muratori, who pointed out several shortcomings of the legal system in an essay entitled *De' difetti della giurisprudenza*. It took a long time, however, for the realization to emerge that not only a few aspects but the whole criminal legislation needed basic reform. An important step forward was the publication, in 1748, of Montesquieu's *Spirit of Laws*. In this work the French writer discussed problems concerning criminal laws from the point of view of an enlightened philosophy. The subject was by no means treated systematically or thoroughly, but Montesquieu's ideas constituted a definite advance toward a more rational and humane conception of the meaning and purpose of penal laws. Besides writing against the use of torture, Montesquieu made several other useful points: he saw the necessity of clearly framed laws; he questioned the usefulness of excessively severe punishments; he supported the principle of a right proportion between crimes and punishments; he expressed the opinion that for purely religious offenses there should be only religious penalties (such as prohibiting attendance at religious ceremonies). For other offenses Montesquieu proposed that, whenever possible, punishments should be of the same nature as crimes. He had no doubt about the necessity of the death penalty: "A citizen deserves death when he has taken, or tried to take, the life of another citizen." All in all, despite the fact that Montesquieu's work was far from comprehensive, one must recognize—as did Beccaria—that he

---

18. For William Penn's attitude in the field of criminal law see Turnbull, *A Visit to the Philadelphia Prison,* pp. 5 ff.

discussed the problem with an open and critical mind, and in this sense he was an important forerunner in the movement for the reform of criminal laws.[19]

Another early reformer was the king of Prussia, Frederick II, whose enlightened ideas were of special importance because, being an absolute ruler, he could put them into effect, thus giving an example of their practical application. While still crown prince, Frederick had recognized the problem of criminal law as worthy of the most serious consideration. Soon after the beginning of his reign in 1740 he abolished torture. A few years later he abrogated the death penalty as a punishment for burglary, and in 1747 he abolished all reprisals against the corpses of persons who had committed suicide. Other reforms were carried out in the following years, always with the purpose of proportioning punishments to the crimes committed. Frederick's actions were not imitated at the time by other rulers, but his ideas and his decisions inspired and encouraged the reform movement.

In France a gross miscarriage of justice moved Voltaire to take a sudden interest in the problem of criminal legislation. In 1762 a man from Toulouse, Jean Calas, after having been convicted of murdering his son, was condemned to be broken on the wheel. Until then Voltaire had concentrated his polemical activity on religious intolerance, which in his opinion was the first cause of almost all man's troubles and miseries. Occasionally he had also criticized certain aspects of the laws, but in rather general terms. The Calas affair turned out to be a decisive event in affecting Voltaire's attitude. His suspicions aroused, he made a personal investigation and found that the young Calas had not been killed by his father, but had committed suicide. He discovered also that the death penalty had been influenced by the fact that Jean Calas was a Protestant and that his son had expressed the intention of becoming a Catholic. As soon as Voltaire became convinced that Calas had been unjustly condemned, he started a campaign for revising the decision of the trial. He wrote a number of pamphlets on the subject, addressed a multitude of letters to eminent persons and to all his friends, and finally, in March of 1763, he succeeded in having the state council order the Toulouse parliament to

---

19. In a letter to his French translator Morellet, Beccaria mentioned Montesquieu's *Persian Letters* (1721) as the first book that influenced him profoundly, but the chapter on criminal problems in Montesquieu's *Spirit of Laws* (1748) was undoubtedly more important for Beccaria's views on penal subjects.

produce all the documents of the trial and the reasons for the sentence. Consequently, the trial was publicized and the decision revised: Jean Calas was declared innocent and his family received from the king a special indemnity.

Although Voltaire's primary intention was still to fight religious intolerance, his victory in the Calas case was a powerful blow to the existing legal system. He had shown how dangerous the secrecy of procedure could be and how this secrecy could lead to arbitrariness and injustice; he had also proclaimed that criminal law was not an exclusive field and that it concerned not only jurists and rulers but the whole of humanity.

From that time on, Voltaire devoted a large part of his activity to the redressing of judicial errors. Although he had no plan for a systematic reform of the criminal legislation, his battles for Calas and other victims of judicial sentences helped to publicize the weakness of the existing system. A question raised by Voltaire, whose reputation was worldwide and who was at the same time greatly revered by his followers and greatly feared by his enemies, could not fail to make an enormous impression on public opinion in all countries.[20]

Although the development of humanistic philosophy in the eighteenth century had already contributed to a more reasonable way of looking at problems and of solving them, the criminal system, with all its prejudices and faults, was so deep-rooted that public opinion had to be stirred energetically before people could be expected to respond and support a thorough reform movement. Voltaire helped in great measure to create this favorable atmosphere: he made people aware that the criminal system was wrong and that innocent men were often condemned to death; he also made clear that another criminal system might be drawn up in spite of the authorities, of the jurists, of tradition, a criminal system which would be less cruel, less arbitrary, more reasonable.

The ground had been prepared. It was now necessary for some clear mind to put the question on a practical plane, showing systematically where the faults were and what the remedies should be. At this auspicious moment appeared the book that answered this need: Beccaria's treatise *On Crimes and Punishments.*

---

20. The most comprehensive work on Voltaire's contributions in the field of criminal laws is Hertz, *Voltaire und die französische Strafrechtspflege im achtzehnten Jahrhundert.*

2

On Crimes and Punishments

In April of 1764 Beccaria's manuscript was sent to the publisher Aubert of Leghorn who had already printed Pietro Verri's *Essay on Happiness*. The first finished copy of Beccaria's treatise—a small book of slightly more than 100 pages—was received in Milan three months later, on July 16, 1764. Neither the name of Beccaria nor that of the printer appeared in the first edition, nor did they appear in two other editions which followed in the next few months. The success of the book was tremendous, and the Patriotic Society of Berne, even before knowing who the author was, decided to award a gold medal to a "citizen who dared to raise his voice in favor of humanity against the most deeply ingrained prejudices."

The secrecy of the book's authorship was short-lived and Beccaria's name did indeed become famous, first in Italy and soon after in the rest of the Western world. A review of the contents of this book will explain the great repercussions—enthusiastic eulogies as well as bitter attacks—which followed its publication.[1]

---

1. For the quotations from Beccaria's treatise *On Crimes and Punishments* the following English translations have been used: Farrer (London, 1880), Paolucci (Indianapolis, 1963), and Kenelm Foster and Jane Grigson (London,

In the introduction Beccaria proclaims the principle which should guide the work of the legislator. The laws, he says, should be enacted with one single purpose in mind: the greatest happiness shared by the greatest number. Already in 1725 the English philosopher Francis Hutcheson had affirmed in his *Inquiry concerning Moral Good and Evil:* "That action is best, which procures the greatest happiness for the greatest numbers; and that worst, which, in like manner, occasions misery." By proclaiming that it is the legislator's responsibility to procure as much happiness as possible to as many people as possible Beccaria carries Hutcheson's formula to what he considers its logical corollary.[2]

While recognizing that progress had been made in many fields during the eighteenth century, Beccaria points out the lack of improvement in the condition of the penal system. Very few men, he says, have studied and fought against the cruelty of punishments and the irregularities of criminal procedures, an aspect of legislation so important and yet so neglected in almost the whole of Europe; and very few men, he adds, have sought to demolish the errors accumulated through the centuries or to curb the ill-directed power which has produced up to now a long series of cold-blooded atrocities.

After mentioning the "great Montesquieu" as the writer who inspired him more than others for the task he has now set for himself, Beccaria states that he will try to discuss the subject with clarity and the weight of evidence, so that penal problems may be solved with "geometrical precision." Far from sure that his statements will be well received, Beccaria concludes his introduction with the words: "If in defending the rights of man and of truth I should help to rescue from the agonies of death one victim of tyranny and ignorance, both equally fatal, the blessings and tears of that single innocent man will console me for the contempt of all mankind."

Beccaria then analyzes the origin of penalties and the right of punishment. Developing Rousseau's theory of the social contract, Beccaria

---

1964). Specific notes referring to the text of the treatise have been omitted, since the description of the contents follows the sequence of chapters in the printed order of the Romagnoli edition.

2. Francis Hutcheson (1694–1746) is known mostly for his ethical writings, among them the *Inquiry concerning Beauty, Order, Harmony, Design* and the *Inquiry concerning Moral Good and Evil,* both first published in 1725. For Hutcheson's formula on happiness see his *Inquiry concerning Moral Good and Evil,* 2d ed., pp. 177–78.

affirms that men, in forming a human society, sacrificed a part of their individual liberty, the least possible portion, in order to enjoy the remainder in peace and security: "The aggregate of these least possible portions constitutes the right of punishment; all that is beyond this is an abuse and not justice, a fact but not a right." A consequence of these principles is that punishments should be fixed by the legislator, who represents the whole society, and that no magistrate (who is a part of society) can, on his own authority, justly inflict punishments upon another member of the same society. This means that there can be no crime and no punishment without a law, that no law can have a retroactive effect and prescribe a punishment for a deed which was not a crime before the enactment of the law, and that the judicial branch of a government cannot have any authority beyond the carrying out of the laws established by the legislative body. Another consequence of these principles is that, should the severity of a punishment prove useless, its maintenance would then be contrary to reason, to justice, and to the nature of the social contract itself.

A final consequence of these principles is that laws should be perfectly clear and precise, rather than arbitrary: according to Beccaria, nothing can be more dangerous than the popular theory that it is necessary to consult "the spirit of the laws." When laws are clearly expressed more people understand them, and "the greater the number of those who understand them and have in their hands the sacred code of the laws, the fewer will be the crimes committed." Beccaria adds: "We can here see how useful the art of printing is which makes the public, and not some few individuals, the guardians of the laws."

Beccaria then comes to discuss another subject: detention pending trial. This measure was completely arbitrary at that time, so that a judge, on a frivolous pretext, was free to deprive a personal enemy of his liberty and to leave a friend at large despite strong proofs of his guilt. Beccaria admits that in many circumstances it is necessary to imprison a man before his conviction, but detention in this case must be determined by the law, not left to the decision of a judge. The law must indicate what evidence should be required to justify the detention of an accused man pending trial, and Beccaria suggests such proofs as an extra-judicial confession, the confession of an accomplice, or the accused man's flight. Beccaria makes it clear, however, that an accused man should not be put in the same jail with convicted criminals, and if this man is finally acquitted, he should be declared free from any mark of infamy.

Beccaria then deals with the evidence used in criminal cases. He is opposed to the system, then in force in most countries, whereby a full proof of guilt is determined by two half-proofs or a number of minor proofs. Only a perfect proof of a crime, says Beccaria, can authorize a condemnation: without certainty of guilt no person should be condemned. Moreover, Beccaria is in favor of everything being open, nothing secret: verdicts should be public, and the proofs of guilt should be public. This is the only way, he maintains, whereby informed opinion, which is the best social restraint, can keep violence and passion in check.

As regards the problem of the persons called upon to give judgment, the principle of the jury system, already established in England, seems to Beccaria preferable to methods adopted in other countries:

> It is a most useful law that everyone shall be judged by his peers, for, where it is a matter of the liberty or the fortune of a citizen, the feelings which inequality inspires should be silent; neither the superiority with which the prosperous man regards the unfortunate, nor the disdain with which the inferior regards the superior, can have any place in a judgment. . . . It also accords with justice that an accused person should have power, up to a certain point, of refusing those whom he may suspect of unfairness toward him.

As regards witnesses, Beccaria argues that the true measure of their credibility is only the interest they have in telling or in not telling the truth; therefore, no evidence should be rejected beforehand.

Beccaria then proceeds to consider the problem of secret accusations, which he describes as "evident, but consecrated abuses, made necessary in many nations by the weakness of the government." Their use, says Beccaria, "makes men false and deceptive, because whoever may suspect that he sees in his neighbor an informer will see in him an enemy." And who, asks Beccaria, "can protect himself from calumny when it is armed with the strongest shield, secrecy? What strange sort of constitution must it be in which the ruler suspects every subject of being an enemy and finds himself compelled, for the sake of public tranquillity, to deprive each man of his personal share in it?" Beccaria admits that this evil practice may sometimes be so deeply ingrained in a national system that an attempt to remove it may seem to precipitate utter ruin; but, he adds, "if I had to dictate new laws in some deserted corner of the universe, before I authorized a custom such as this, my hand would tremble and I would have all posterity before my eyes."

On the subject of oaths Beccaria asserts that he is against imposing them on the accused:

> Laws and the natural sentiments of man contradict one another when oaths are administered to the accused, binding him to be truthful when he can best serve his own interests by being false; as if a man could really swear to contribute to his own destruction; as if religion were not silent in most men when interest speaks. . . . The affairs of heaven are regulated by laws altogether different from those that govern human affairs. Why compromise one with the other? Why place men in the terrible dilemma of either sinning against God or concurring in their own ruin?

The next chapter deals with the problem of torture, and Beccaria reaffirms with great strength the viewpoint of the most enlightened people who had preceded him, adding some eloquent arguments of his own:

> Torture is a sure method for the acquittal of robust scoundrels and for the condemnation of innocent but feeble men. . . . The examination of an accused person is undertaken to ascertain the truth. But if the truth is difficult to discover from a man's air, demeanor, or countenance when he is at ease, how much more difficult will it be to discover it from a man whose face is distorted by pain. . . . A strange consequence that necessarily follows from the use of torture is that the innocent person is placed in a condition worse than that of the guilty: under torture an innocent man either confesses the crime and is unjustly condemned, or he is declared innocent, having suffered an undeserved punishment. The guilty man has, instead, one chance in his favor, since, if he resists the torture firmly and is acquitted, he has escaped a greater punishment by enduring a lesser one. Therefore, the innocent man can only lose, the guilty man may gain.

Beccaria also gives an argument against torture which is based on the principle that a man is innocent until proved guilty. A man cannot be called guilty, he says, until he has been sentenced by the judge; what right, then, has the judge to inflict punishment on a citizen while his guilt or his innocence remains in doubt? The crime is either certain or uncertain: if certain, no other punishment should be inflicted other than the one established by law; if uncertain, it is wrong to torture an innocent man, since he must be considered innocent as long as his guilt has not been proved.

But what about torture that might be used to make a criminal reveal his accomplices in the crime? "If we have proved," says Beccaria, "that torture is a bad method for discovering the truth, how can it serve to reveal the accomplices, which is one of the truths to be discovered?" And Beccaria concludes his chapter on torture by singling out the nations where its use had never been adopted or had been discontinued: England in the first place, Sweden, and also Prussia (described as the country "where one of the wisest monarchs of Europe has taken philosophy with him to the throne"). Torture, Beccaria observes finally, is not deemed necessary in the laws that regulate armies. How strange, he says, "that the laws of peace should have to learn a more humane method of judgment from spirits hardened to slaughter and bloodshed!"

Beccaria then proceeds to discuss matters connected with the prosecution of arrested persons. Trials, he says, should be held with the least possible delay because promptness of punishment is one of the most effective checks against crime. Of course, time should be allowed for the accused to prepare his defense and for the prosecution to prepare the case against him. The law, and not the judge, should fix this time according to the type of crime and other factors. Beccaria says that the law must be as precise as possible and that arbitrariness should be reduced to the absolute minimum. As regards a time limit for the prosecution of crimes, Beccaria is in favor of some limitations for minor crimes; but, he adds, "those atrocious crimes which are long remembered should not, when they have been proved, merit any limitation in favor of the criminal who has spared himself by flight."

In discussing criminal attempts Beccaria then says: "Laws do not punish intent; but surely an act undertaken with the manifest intention of committing a crime deserves punishment, though less than that which is due upon the actual execution of the crime. The importance of preventing a criminal attempt authorizes punishment, but since there may be an interval between the attempt and the execution, the greater punishment established for the accomplished crime may lead to repentance."

As regards the question of impunity, Beccaria notes that some tribunals offer impunity to the accomplice in a major crime if he will reveal the names of his companions. Such an expedient, says Beccaria, has disadvantages as well as advantages. One disadvantage is that the nation authorizes treachery, an evil even when practiced by scoundrels; another disadvantage is that the tribunal admits its own uncertainty and the weakness of its law when it has to ask help from the one who breaks it. On the other hand, the offer of impunity has the advantage of making it possible to prosecute criminals who otherwise would not be apprehended. Should then impunity be accepted? Beccaria appears rather hesitant: "At any rate it seems to me that a general law promising impunity to an accomplice who reveals the details of a crime would be preferable to special arrangements in particular cases."

And so we come to one of the fundamental chapters in Beccaria's book, the one dealing with the problem of punishments. Although subscribing to the principle that punishment should be duly proportioned to the crime, Beccaria rejects the theory of retribution as the reason for punishing:

> The purpose of punishments is neither to torture a man nor to undo a crime already committed. . . . The object of punishment is simply to prevent the criminal from injuring anew his fellow citizens and to deter others from committing similar injuries. Therefore, those punishments and that method of inflicting them should be chosen which, in due proportion to the offense, will produce the strongest and most lasting impression on the minds of men, and inflict the least torment on the body of the criminal. . . . In order that a punishment may attain its object it is enough if the harm of the punishment exceeds the advantage of the crime, and in this excess of harm the certainty of punishment and the loss of the possible advantage from the crime should be included; all beyond this is superfluous and consequently tyrannical.

Beccaria sees a relationship between the state of a nation and the scale of punishments. He is convinced that the abolition of cruel and ferocious punishments would contribute to making the people of a nation more humane and sensitive, and therefore would tend to reduce the number and the atrocity of crimes. Beccaria is in favor of imprisonment as a civilized method for punishing a criminal, and for the most serious crimes he prescribes perpetual servitude. In fact, and this is the most daring proposal in his book, Beccaria takes a stand against the death penalty. Not only does he deny any justification for capital punishment, but he seems to go so far as to challenge the right of men to kill other men for any reason, thus upholding in its entirety the old commandment, "Thou shalt not kill."

"I want to examine," begins Beccaria, "if the death penalty is really just and useful in a well-organized state." By what right, he asks, do men kill other men? Certainly not the right from which the laws themselves derive because they represent the general will, which is the aggregate of particular wills; and who ever wished to leave to other men the option of killing him? We say that man has no right to kill himself; but how can we admit that he gave to others or to the entire society the right to kill him? Therefore, the punishment of death is not a right. But, continues Beccaria, it may nevertheless be deemed useful or necessary. "There are only two possible motives," he says, "for believing that the death of a citizen is necessary. The first is when, though deprived of his personal freedom, he still has such connections and power as to threaten the national security and produce a dangerous revolution." Therefore, the death of this citizen, says Beccaria, may be deemed necessary only in time of anarchy, when disorders have taken the place of the law, and it is clear that this situation does not arise in a nation governed by laws and supported by public opinion. The second reason for destroying a citizen, continues Beccaria, would be that of deterring others from committing crimes. But, Beccaria explains, "the greatest effect that any punishment has upon the human mind is not to be measured by its intensity but by its duration, for our sensibility is more easily and permanently affected by slight but repeated impressions than by a strong but brief shock. . . . It is not the terrible yet momentary spectacle of the death of a wretch, but the long and painful example of a man deprived of liberty for the rest of his life which is the strongest deterrent."

Beccaria has thus shown that the death penalty is neither just nor useful or necessary. He seems fearful, however, that his demonstration could be challenged and, therefore, appealing to the conscience of mankind, he gives another and more eloquent reason for the abolition of the death penalty:

> Capital punishment cannot be useful because of the example of barbarity it presents. If human passions or the necessities of war have taught men to shed one another's blood, the laws, which are intended to moderate human conduct, ought not to extend the savage example,

which in the case of a legal execution is all the more baneful in that it is carried out with studied formalities. To me it seems an absurdity that the laws, which are the expression of the public will, which abhor and which punish murder, should themselves commit one; and that, to deter citizens from private assassination, they should themselves order a public murder. . . . What are every man's feelings about capital punishment? Let us read them in the gestures of indignation and scorn with which everyone looks upon the executioner, who is, after all, an innocent administrator of the public will, a good citizen contributing to the public welfare, an instrument as necessary for the internal security of a nation as brave soldiers are for the external. What, then, is the source of this contradiction? And why is this feeling, in spite of reason, ineradicable in mankind? Because man in the most secret recesses of his heart, that part which more than any other still preserves the original form of nature, has always believed that his life lies in the power of no one, except destiny alone which, with its iron scepter, rules the universe. . . . And if it will be objected that in almost all ages and in almost all nations some crimes have been punished by death, I shall reply that this objection does not mean anything because the history of mankind appears as a vast sea of errors, among which a few confused truths are to be found. . . . The fact that very few societies, and only for a very brief time, have abstained from applying the death penalty is more favorable than harmful to my case, since it shares the fate of all great truths which appear as flashes in the long dark night in which mankind is enveloped. The happy time has not yet arrived in which truth shall be the possession of the greater number, as error has been so far.

This, then, is Beccaria's plea for the abolition of capital punishment. We may say here that later in life Beccaria added another reason for the abolition of the death penalty when in 1792, as a member of the commission for the reform of the criminal system of Lombardy, he pointed out that the death penalty is irrevocable and without remedy in case of a judicial error.

In this chapter Beccaria does not discuss his attitude toward war, but his feeling is implied in the questions: "By what right do men kill other men?" and "Who ever wished to leave to other men the option of killing him?" Beccaria also speaks of the "savage example" taught by the "necessities of war." It seems fairly clear, therefore, that Beccaria was opposed to any killing of man by man and that he was essentially a man of peace.

The subsequent chapters of Beccaria's book deal with other types of penalties, such as banishment and confiscation. Stressing once more the importance of swiftness in the conviction of criminals, Beccaria says that in the minds of potential criminals the seductive idea of an advantageous crime should always be associated with that of its prompt punishment. The knowledge that punishment is unavoidable is, in Beccaria's opinion, the greatest preventive of crime; therefore, together with a mild system of laws must go the certainty of punishments. A pardon, in Beccaria's view, "is the tacit mark of disapproval that a ruler exhibits toward a code." Showing men that crimes may be pardoned and that punishment is not their necessary consequence encourages the hope of impunity and creates the belief that sentences, which might be remitted and are not, are "violent exhibitions of force rather than emanations of justice."

The same reason that makes Beccaria oppose the granting of pardons makes him oppose any possibility for a criminal to find asylum in his own or in any other country. Referring to the ecclesiastical privilege of granting asylum to escaping criminals, Beccaria says: "Within the confines of a country there should be no place independent of the laws; their power should follow every citizen, as the shadow follows the body . . . and since the effect of punishments depends more on their certainty than on their severity, asylums encourage crimes more than punishments deter them." As regards criminals who escape to other countries, Beccaria thinks that in principle they should be subject to extradition and be brought to justice in the country of their misdeeds. Beccaria hesitates, however, to support an international pact on extradition before the adoption by all nations of moderate and just laws. As long as in some countries men face absurd and cruel punishments, their deportation may be a cruel act in itself; but Beccaria is convinced that a general convention on extradition would be a desirable goal once just laws were established everywhere. In that case, he says, "the certainty that there is not a square foot of soil in which true crimes are left unpunished would be a most efficacious means of preventing them."

Beccaria then explains why a just proportion between crimes and punishments is so necessary. It is in the common interest, he says, not only that crimes not be committed, but also that they be less frequent in proportion to the harm they cause society. Therefore, the obstacles that deter men from committing crimes should be stronger when the crimes are more harmful to the public good. Moreover, it is clear that if the same penalty were given for stealing a pheasant and for killing a man, the difference between these crimes in the minds of the people would cease to exist, and the moral feelings which have evolved slowly through many centuries and with much difficulty would be destroyed.

Having made it clear that the only true measure of crime is the harm done to society, Beccaria states that the same code should apply to all members of society, regardless of wealth or rank. It must be noted in this respect that in Beccaria's time equality before the law was often only theoretical and in some cases not even theoretical because of special privileges in favor of noblemen and of some members of the clergy. "The great and rich," says Beccaria, "should not have any advantage over the less fortunate, wealth should never nourish tyranny. . . . There is no liberty whenever the laws permit that in certain circumstances a man, because he is weak or poor, ceases to be a *person* and becomes a *thing*."

As regards noblemen in particular, Beccaria explains that it is not his intention to inquire whether the hereditary distinction between nobles and commoners is useful. He will assert only that punishments should be exactly the same for the first as for the least citizen:

> To the objection that the same punishment inflicted on a nobleman and a plebeian is not really the same because of the diversity of their education, and because of the disgrace that is spread over an illustrious family, I would answer that the measure of punishments is not the sensibility of the criminal, but the public injury, which is all the more grave when committed by a person of rank; that equality of punishments can only be extrinsic, since in reality the effect on each individual is different; finally, that the disgrace of a family may be removed by the sovereign through public demonstration of benevolence toward the innocent relatives of the criminal.

Beccaria then proceeds to examine various types of crimes and he makes clear, first of all, that there should be no attempt to confuse human and divine justice. Men cannot judge or punish those who sin against God, says Beccaria, because God, being perfect, has reserved to himself the right to be legislator and judge at the same time. Apparently having in mind the activity of the Inquisition, still strong in several European countries, Beccaria says: "If God has decreed eternal punishments for those who disobey his omnipotence, what insect shall dare to take the place of divine justice, or shall wish to avenge that Being who is all-sufficient to himself, who can receive from things no impression of pleasure or pain, and who alone of all beings acts without reaction?"

Beccaria then turns to one class of crimes—thefts and robberies. As usual, he is particularly concerned about the sacredness of human life, and he makes a clear distinction between simple thefts and those accompanied by assault and violence. For these he would reserve severe punishments, since human lives would be imperiled; but simple thefts, says Beccaria, are often the consequence of poverty and despair, crimes "committed by those to whom the right of property, a terrible and perhaps unnecessary right, has left very little." For these crimes Beccaria proposes fines or short prison terms. It is interesting to see this young member of the Milanese aristocracy foreshadow future socialist doctrines and express doubts about the legitimacy of the right of property. In fact, as we will soon see, Beccaria returned to this subject a few years later, when he dealt with economic problems.

It may seem strange that a humanist like Beccaria should consider suicide a crime. It has been suggested that this was, perhaps, a concession to religious groups, but another explanation is probably better founded. In his chapter on the death penalty Beccaria had stated: "We say that man has no right to kill himself, but how can we admit that he gave to others the right to kill him?" It is clear that Beccaria's opposition to the death penalty would be weakened by his recognition that man does have the right to take his own life. In any case Beccaria is quick to add that in the case of suicide any punishment is inadmissible because it would fall either on the innocent relatives of the person who committed suicide or else upon a cold and insensitive body. "This latter punishment," says Beccaria, "couldn't make more impression on the living than would be made by inflicting violence on a statue; and to punish the relatives would be unjust and tyrannical, inasmuch as political freedom necessarily presupposes the purely personal nature of punishments."

There is one class of crimes that Beccaria says he does not want to discuss, alluding to the so-called crimes of heresy whereby people were prosecuted for expressing thoughts contrary to the prevailing beliefs:

> The reader of this work will notice that I have omitted a class of
> crimes that has covered Europe with human blood and has raised

those woeful pyres of living human bodies in times when this was a pleasant spectacle and the ignorant crowds rejoiced in hearing the muffled, confused groans that came out of the vortices of black smoke, the smoke of human flesh, together with the crackling of charred bones and the frying of still palpitating entrails.

Beccaria then adds with obvious irony:

Reasonable men will see that the place, the age, and the subject treated here do not permit me to examine the nature of such a crime; it would take me too long and too far afield to prove that a perfect uniformity of thought is necessary in a state . . . and that opinions, distinguished by the subtlest and obscurest differences, may neverthe-less upset public order when one belief is not authorized in prefer-ence to the others. . . . It would also be too complicated to prove that, however odious the imposition of force upon human minds, none-theless it must be accepted . . . provided this is done by someone with acknowledged authority.

By his words Beccaria shows, of course, that he is in favor of freedom of conscience and against authoritarian methods of thought control. According to some critics, fear of persecution may have con-tributed to Beccaria's sarcastic and indirect approach to this subject. We should not exclude this possibility, although it seems that Beccaria could hardly expect anyone not to see clearly what he had in mind.

In the last chapter of his book Beccaria examines ways of prevent-ing crimes. "It is better to prevent crimes than to punish them," he says, "and this should be the main purpose of good legislation." Bec-caria suggests several ways of preventing crimes, besides having a code of good and clear laws, known and understood by the greatest number of people. He is convinced, for example, that it would be useful if the magistrates who carry out the laws were led to observe them rather than to corrupt them. He suggests that the number of men who compose the magistracy be increased because venality is less likely among men who are under the close observation of their colleagues. Beccaria also proposes that virtue be rewarded. This prac-tice, he says, has never been adopted; but if the prizes awarded by literary and scientific academies have contributed to the publication of good books and to an increase of useful knowledge, why not award prizes for virtuous deeds? Finally, says Beccaria, the surest but most difficult means of preventing crime is to improve education; but he adds that this is too vast a subject and one that goes beyond the limits he has set for himself. He makes clear in any case that for education he does not mean an accumulation of sterile notions, but a selection of creative ideas and thoughts which would lead young people toward a better and more virtuous life.

Beccaria concludes:

From all I have written one may deduce a general theorem of great utility, though hardly conformable with custom, the usual legislator of nations. The theorem is this: *In order for a punishment not to be an act of violence of one or of many against a private citizen, it ought to be public, prompt, necessary, the minimum possible in the given circumstances, proportionate to the crime, dictated by the laws.*

3

The Success of
the Treatise

Beccaria himself was very much surprised by the interest that his treatise *On Crimes and Punishments* aroused everywhere. What made his book so important? Certainly not all his ideas were new: torture had been condemned by other writers, the right proportion between crimes and punishments had already been recognized by others as a necessary principle of criminal law, and various voices had been raised against the secrecy of procedure and in favor of clear and precise laws. Moreover, the idea of the social contract giving the right to punish, although changed to other proportions, came from Hobbes and Rousseau. But along with the reaffirmation of claims already made by others Beccaria added many new ones, of which the most important for its revolutionary character was the proposal to abolish the death penalty. Moreover, the great merit of Beccaria's book— and this explains its great success and the practical impact that it would soon have in many countries—lies in the fact that for the first time the principles of a penal reform were expressed in a systematic and concise way, and the rights of humanity were defended in the clearest terms, with the most logical arguments. In the eighteenth century, just as in other times, juridical books were often written in an almost incomprehensible language where only the specialists would find themselves at home; and here, instead, came a thin volume written by a young man in a simple and unpretentious style that could be read and understood by any cultivated person.

Beccaria's book had other qualities besides clarity and logic. It was a highly eloquent cry of revolt against tyranny, cruelty, absurdities, and abuses; and what gave strength to this cry were Beccaria's sincere sympathy for the most unfortunate and unjustly treated sections of humanity and his earnest desire to see the triumph of real justice in a more civilized society.

While the book was being received with great enthusiasm in the enlightened circles of Milan and other cities, traditional jurists and religious groups were quick to attack it. One of the first and most violent pamphlets attacking Beccaria was that of Father Facchinei, a Vallombrosian monk, who apparently launched his assault under the pressure of the inquisitorial Council of Ten in Venice which had resented Beccaria's criticism of secret accusations. Facchinei's book, entitled *Notes and Observations on the Book "On Crimes and Punishments,"* was published in Venice at the beginning of January 1765, just a few months after the publication of Beccaria's treatise.[1]

Distorting many of Beccaria's viewpoints and theories, Facchinei wrote a tract containing six charges of sedition and twenty-three of irreligion. Here are a few samples of Facchinei's prose:

> The author of the book *On Crimes and Punishments* does not know that kind of justice which originates from the eternal legislator who sees and foresees everything.
>
> All sensible people have found that the author of the book *On Crimes and Punishments* is an enemy of Christianity, a wicked man and a poor philosopher.
>
> He is a declared enemy of the Supreme Being.
>
> He stresses the fact that Christianity has been responsible for some suffering and loss of life, but does not say a word about the advantages that the lights of the Gospels have spread over all mankind.
>
> He describes in hateful colors the religious orders, especially the monks.
>
> He accuses the prelates of the Catholic church, well known for

---

1. The title of Facchinei's book in Italian was *Note e osservazioni sul libro dei delitti e delle pene.* Facchinei's first name was Ferdinando, not Angelo or Vincenzo as erroneously indicated by some writers.

their benign and charitable feelings, of inflicting penalties that are as unjust as they are barbarous.

He refuses to consider heresy a crime against God. He affirms that heretics are victims of some linguistic subtleties.

He writes sacrilegious impostures against the Inquisition.

He considers all princes and monarchs of this century as cruel tyrants.

He affirms that the interest of the individual is more important than that of society in general or of those who represent it.

He states that a monarch has no right to inflict the death penalty.

This language may seem too intemperate to be taken seriously. But it was taken seriously by many, among them Beccaria himself, who knew very well that the party of the intolerants was still powerful and dangerous despite the fact that the Inquisition of the Roman church in Lombardy had been officially abolished. Beccaria was suddenly seized by fear: he wanted to defend humanity without becoming a martyr, as he would soon confess to André Morellet. The Verri brothers came to the rescue of their friend. Not being directly involved they remained cool, and composed in a few days a defense of the treatise, written in the first person as if it were Beccaria himself writing. Entitled *Apology of the book "On Crimes and Punishments,"* it was promptly sent to the Leghorn printer; it answered point by point all of Facchinei's accusations. There also were some light touches of humor in the answers to Facchinei: for example, to the accusation that the author of the book had depicted religious orders and monks in hateful colors, the reply was: "It would be difficult to find a passage in the book in which any reference is made to religious orders or monks—unless one interprets in an arbitrary manner some thoughts about idleness."[2]

But neither reason nor touches of humor would have saved Beccaria from trouble if the head of the Milan administration, Count Carlo Firmian, had not intervened personally in Beccaria's favor and had not nipped in the bud all attempts at persecution. Firmian had read the book as soon as it appeared and had liked it. In fact, he wrote a note saying that he felt flattered by what he had read because

---

2. For more details about Facchinei's book and the answer written by the Verri brothers in Beccaria's name see Beccaria, *Des délits et des peines,* ed. Collin de Plancy, pp. 399 ff.; also Cantù, pp. 56–57, and Beccaria, *Dei delitti e delle pene,* ed. Venturi, pp. 164–86. The Italian title of the *Apology* was *Apologia al libro "Dei delitti e delle pene."*

he himself had entertained similar ideas on the matters discussed. "The book," he said, "seems to have been written with great love for mankind and with great imagination." Firmian also wrote to the court of Vienna to praise the book and to say that it did honor to its author.

We may mention here a curious fact which was pointed out by the Italian historian Franco Venturi. Having done some research on the origin of the words *socialism* and *socialist,* Venturi discovered that they were probably used for the first time—in their Italian forms *socialismo* and *socialista*—by none other than Father Facchinei in his attack on Beccaria. In fact, according to Venturi, Facchinei coined the term *socialist* and used it to describe the ideas of equalitarianism and utilitarianism that he had perceived as the base of Beccaria's theories. To be sure, Beccaria's doubts about the legitimacy of the right of property anticipated socialist views and, although Facchinei's use of the term was still rather vague, Beccaria was very likely the first man to be accused of being a socialist.[3]

Facchinei's invectives against Beccaria were not simply the outburst of a fanatical individual, as some may think. The reaction of the Roman church itself to Beccaria's ideas was made clear when, in February 1766, the treatise *On Crimes and Punishments* was placed on the Index of condemned books, having been found too close to the rationalistic philosophy; and it remained on that list until the Index itself was abolished by the Ecumenical Council convoked by Pope John XXIII in 1962. In the *Enciclopedia Cattolica* an article on Beccaria by Oliviero Savini Nicci, written in 1949, gave a contradictory appraisal of the book and its author, justifying the official condemnation and at the same time giving credit to Beccaria for his contribution to useful penal reforms. More recently, in 1967, the *New Catholic Encyclopedia,* published in the United States under the sponsorship of the Catholic University of America, was less ambiguous. An article by R. Lane stated clearly that Beccaria contributed "more than any other" to the penal reforms of the eighteenth century. The article added that Beccaria was in the mainstream of rationalistic thought, but no adverse criticism accompanied this statement. Therefore, judging by this recent indication, it would seem that a more objec-

---

3. See *Accademia delle Scienze di Torino, Atti del Convegno internazionale su Cesare Beccaria, Memorie—Classe di scienze morali, serie IV, no. 9* (lecture by Venturi, "Beccaria e la sua fortuna," p. 9).

tive view has replaced the old opposition of the Church toward Beccaria's theories.

First Contact with French Writers

Even more surprising to us may seem the attacks on Beccaria by some famous jurists, such as the Frenchmen Muyart de Vouglans and Daniel Jousse. The former, in a *Letter of Refutation,* published in 1767, defended the existing penal system and concentrated his arguments on torture which, he said, had proved its usefulness during many centuries in practically all nations; he added: "If two or three countries have discarded the use of torture, they are the exception which confirms the general rule." As for Daniel Jousse, he listed in the introduction to his *Treatise on French Criminal Justice* (published in 1771, but undoubtedly written earlier) the principal books on legal subjects, adding to these the title of Beccaria's book with the following remark: "I would not mention this book if many people had not commented on it approvingly and had not spoken of it in very good terms; but the most sensible people have judged otherwise. . . . In fact, this book, instead of throwing some light on the matter of crimes and punishments, tends on the contrary to establish a very dangerous system and to introduce new ideas which, if they were adopted, would simply overthrow the laws accepted up to now by the best-governed states and would endanger religion, morality, and the most sacred rules of government."[4]

Why these attacks on Beccaria on the part of the jurists? Perhaps Daniel Jousse unwittingly gave the reason for their attitude in those two words "new ideas." Beccaria's book had suddenly brought fresh air into the stale atmosphere of tradition. The men who had built their lives, their fortunes, and their reputations on the old customs could not bear to see this young idealist suddenly ruin their edifice.

It must be said, however, that the success of Beccaria's book was not impaired by these attacks. On the contrary, this opposition favored rather than harmed the spreading of Beccaria's theories, to which the attention of Europe was gradually being drawn by the innumerable discussions they raised. Some early reactions to the new book came

---

4. The full title in French of Muyart de Vouglans's pamphlet was *Lettre concernant la réfutation de quelques principes hasardés dans le "Traité des délits et des peines."* The French title of Jousse's treatise was *Traité de la justice criminelle de France.*

from France where already in February 1765 a brief review of Beccaria's treatise appeared in the *Gazette littéraire de l'Europe,* a Parisian periodical directed by Jean-Baptiste Suard. Further comments on Beccaria's work appeared a few months later in the same *Gazette,* as well as in the *Correspondance littéraire,* a handwritten newsletter directed by Melchior Grimm and regularly sent twice a month to a few selected subscribers (among them Catherine II of Russia, the king of Poland, and several German princes).[5]

Around that time, still in the first months of 1765, Beccaria's friend, the mathematician Paolo Frisi, sent a copy of the treatise *On Crimes and Punishments* to Jean Le Rond D'Alembert, also a mathematician and one of the leading humanists in Paris. D'Alembert understood the importance of the book and urged the Abbé Morellet, like him a collaborator on the *Encyclopédie,* to translate the book into French.[6]

Beccaria received this news from Frisi with great joy and promptly, on August 24, 1765, wrote a letter to D'Alembert, thanking him for his intervention and indicating some changes to be made in the text. On January 3, 1766, about a year and a half after the publication of the first Italian edition of the treatise *On Crimes and Punishments,* Morellet sent Beccaria a copy of the book in French and wrote him a long letter in which he gave reasons for some changes in the

---

5. The *Gazette littéraire de l'Europe* lasted about three years, from 1764 through 1766. Besides reviewing Beccaria's treatise, the *Gazette* mentioned in its issues Pietro Verri's *Essay on Happiness* and printed in translation two of *Il Caffè*'s articles, the "Spirit of Italian Literature" by Pietro Verri and the "Fragment on Style" by Beccaria (see Venturi, pp. 740–41). For the text of the reviews of Beccaria's book in the *Gazette littéraire de l'Europe* and in the *Correspondance littéraire* see Beccaria, *Dei delitti e delle pene,* ed. Venturi, pp. 310–12, 315–22, 338–45, 369–71. Jean-Baptiste Suard (1733–1817), a skillful journalist and writer, directed the *Gazette* in cooperation with François Arnaud.

Frédéric (or Friedrich) Melchior Grimm (1723–1807) was born in Germany, but settled in Paris and wrote in French. His *Correspondance littéraire* was quite successful and lasted until 1773. Grimm then lived for some time in Russia and enjoyed the protection of Catherine II.

6. André Morellet (1727–1819) had been praised highly by Voltaire for having published in 1761 a critical tract on the Inquisition. Jean Le Rond D'Alembert (1717–83) was the author of several scientific treatises, including one on dynamics and another on the causes of winds.

D'Alembert spoke of Beccaria's book in his letters to Frisi of June 21 and July 9, 1765 (see Landry, *Cesare Beccaria—Scritti e lettere inediti,* p. 107). Beccaria thought that only D'Alembert had urged Morellet to translate his book, but apparently another admirer, M. de Malesherbes, had also encouraged Morellet to translate it (see Landry, pp. 115 ff.).

arrangement of the chapters, telling him that this edition had already had a very great success in France. Here are some passages of Morellet's letter to Beccaria:

Sir, without having the honor of being known by you, I take the liberty of sending you a copy of my translation of your book *On Crimes and Punishments.* Men of letters belong to all nations and to the whole world; they are united by links stronger than those which exist among the citizens of one country, the inhabitants of one city, the members of one family. For this reason I hope that you will not refuse to have with me an exchange of ideas and sentiments that I will treasure very highly. . . . M. D'Alembert, to whom I am bound by a close friendship, lent me your book last June, and I read it with enthusiasm. He asked me to translate it into our language. To be sure, I didn't need any urging; I translated it and I read my translation to M. D'Alembert and to some other men of letters who knew and admired the original. . . . It is now eight days since my translation has been published. I did not write you sooner because I wanted to tell you about the reception that your book would have here. I can now assure you, dear sir, that the success is universal; not only is there an exceptional interest in your book, but the general feeling toward the author couldn't be more flattering. . . . I have been asked to transmit to you the compliments and the grateful expressions of M. Diderot, M. Helvétius, and M. de Buffon. I will soon let you know some of the remarks made by M. Diderot as a result of our discussions. . . . I also gave a copy of your book to M. Rousseau who stopped in Paris on his way to England. . . . Mr. Hume, who has been living in Paris in recent years, has also asked me to send you his best regards. I don't need to mention M. D'Alembert who must have written to you already. . . . In fact, may I say that if it is at all possible for you to travel to France, you should come here to accept personally the proofs of esteem and admiration that you so amply deserve. I entreat you to come to Paris in my name and on behalf of all the people I have just mentioned. . . . I am very impatient to receive your answer and to have your judgment about my translation.

The rest of Morellet's letter was taken up by some questions about Beccaria himself, by details concerning the translation, and by some information on Morellet's own publications.

The great satisfaction that Beccaria felt in receiving Morellet's letter is shown in his answer, written very promptly on January 26, 1766. It is a warm and friendly letter, and some passages are worth quoting:

Your delightful letter has produced in me deep feelings of friendship and gratitude. I cannot tell you how honored I feel in seeing my work translated into the language of a nation which is the guide and illuminator of Europe. I myself owe everything to French books. They first developed in my soul feelings of humanity which had been stifled by eight years of a fanatical education. I already admired you for the excellent articles that you wrote for the great *Encyclopédie* and it was for me the most pleasant surprise to see that a famous man like you was willing to translate my treatise. I thank you with all my heart and I really think that by your translation you have improved on the original. Also the order that you gave to the chapters is more natural and I will follow it myself for future editions. . . .[7]

It is true that, having in mind what happened to Machiavelli, to Galilei and Giannone, I have been obscure in some passages of my book, but the fact is that I wanted to defend humanity without becoming a martyr. It was also a question of inexperience, perhaps forgivable in an author who is now but twenty-eight and who started writing only five years ago. . . . [8]

I was very touched by the words of those illustrious men mentioned in your letter: D'Alembert, Diderot, Helvétius, Buffon, Hume, names which no one can hear without emotion. Their immortal works are the object of my continual study, of my occupation by day and of my meditation in the silence of night. I feel that I have been compensated beyond all my hopes by receiving praises from these great men. . . .

I am very flattered by your curiosity about myself. My family has some wealth, and I am the oldest son; but certain circumstances, some unavoidable and some determined by the will of someone else, did not make my life easy. I have a father whose old age and prejudices I must respect. I am married to a young and sensitive woman, eager to improve her spiritual education, to whom I am attached by a tender affection. As for me, my main interest is to study philosophy in peace and thus to satisfy three very strong feelings of mine: love of literary fame, love of freedom, and compassion for the misfortunes of men, slaves of so many errors. My conversion to philosophy dates back only five years, and I owe it to my reading of the

---

7. Contrary to his statement to Morellet, Beccaria seems to have had second thoughts and did not change the order of chapters in the future Italian editions. In France itself Morellet's arrangement found little favor, as shown by Diderot's and Grimm's reactions (see Beccaria, *Dei delitti e delle pene,* ed. Venturi, pp. 338–45, p. 405).

8. Pietro Giannone (1676–1748) was an Italian historian who had been persecuted and jailed for having criticized in his books the policies of the Catholic church.

The inclusion of Machiavelli in Beccaria's list of victims of persecution is rather strange because Machiavelli's imprisonment had nothing to do with freedom of conscience; it was simply an act of revenge on the part of his political enemies.

Persian Letters. The second work that made a great impression on my soul was that of Helvétius. He led me on the path of truth and revealed to me the blindness and the pitfalls of mankind; to his *Esprit* I owe many of my ideas. The sublime work of Buffon opened to me the sanctuary of nature, and I was impressed by all the writings of Diderot. . . . My spirit was enthralled and enlightened by the profound metaphysics of Hume, by the truth and novelty of his views; I read recently with infinite pleasure the eighteen volumes of his history and I saw in him a political writer, a philosopher and a historian of the highest order. . . . As to M. D'Alembert, I have enough knowledge of mathematics to regard him as the greatest geometer of our century. . . .

I lead a tranquil and solitary life if we can call solitude a small society of friends whose souls and hearts are in continuous motion. We share the same studies and the same pleasures. This activity prevents me from feeling like an exile in my own country. This city is still buried under the prejudices left by its old masters. The Milanese do not forgive those who would like to make them live in the eighteenth century. In this capital city of 120,000 people there are no more than twenty persons who would like to increase their knowledge and who love truth and virtue. Our group of friends, convinced of the educational possibilities of periodical publications, has been printing one that has as its model the English *Spectator*. I will send you a collection of the issues we have published, and you will see some of my articles. . . . Some of the articles are by Pietro Verri, my best friend, a superior man for his qualities of heart and mind. He encouraged me to write and I owe it to him that I didn't throw the manuscript of my *Crimes and Punishments* in the fire; he himself copied it for me with his own hand. . . .

I would rush to Paris if I had the means to do so. . . . I hope, however, that the situation will change and that this delay will enable me to become worthier of your company and of that of your illustrious friends. . . . In the meantime please consider me your correspondent in Italy for anything you may need, and I will be glad to do the same for all your friends. . . . I will tell Count Firmian all the things you have asked me to. He has protected my book and I owe to him my present serenity.

These are the most significant parts of Beccaria's first letter to Morellet. Their correspondence continued after this first exchange and the friendship between the two men became well established. The French translation of Beccaria's book had even more success than the original Italian: seven French editions were published in the first six months and the author's fame then spread quickly to other countries.[9]

In spite of some hostility from professional men, new editions were rapidly succeeding one another in several languages. A first English translation under the title *An Essay on Crimes and Punishments* appeared in London in 1767, published by J. Almon; another English edition was published in the same year in Dublin by J. Exshaw. Other English editions appeared in the next few years, including some printed in North America (the first probably in Charleston, S.C., in 1777).[10]

German, Dutch, Polish, and Spanish translations were published at the time of the first English edition or soon after. Some years later Beccaria's book appeared in Greek and Russian, as well as in other languages, so that the total number of editions before the end of the century had already climbed to about sixty. Several well-known writers commented on and annotated Beccaria's book. Blackstone quoted from Beccaria's treatise the very year after its publication, while Diderot and Morellet added their notes to some of the French editions of the book.

Diderot in his comments agreed with the book's general thesis; however, he had some reservations not only about the abolition of the death penalty, but, strangely enough, even about the use of torture, which Diderot argued might be necessary for the discovery of accomplices. He added that he would favor its use only on a convicted

---

9. The first French edition of Beccaria's book bore the heading: *"Traité des délits et des peines,"* traduit de l'Italien, d'après la troisième édition, revue, corrigée et augmentée par l'Auteur. It was published in Paris without any mention of author, translator, or publisher. The place of publication was indicated as Lausanne. Fictitious places of publication were given also in the next editions. All this shows that the atmosphere for enlightened ideas in France was still unfriendly (see Landry, p. 24).

10. The Charleston edition of Beccaria's treatise, like many other English editions, contained also Voltaire's *Commentary;* it was "printed and sold by David Bruce, at his shop in Church Street, Charlestown." Charles Evans's *American Bibliography* lists tentatively an earlier American edition of Beccaria's treatise on the basis of an advertisement in *Rivington's New York Gazetteer* of October 28, 1773, announcing the forthcoming publication of Beccaria's *Essay on Crimes and Punishments*. However, since no trace seems to exist of this edition, it would seem that the project was not carried out. Therefore, the Charleston edition of Beccaria's treatise was most likely the first to be published in America.

criminal when all other means were exhausted. It is difficult to understand how an enlightened man like Diderot did not see that torture is a degrading act per se. We know, of course, that in our own day and in the most civilized countries the accused is often tormented in order to extort from him confessions as to accomplices, but this is an abuse which, however useful it may seem in a particular case, cannot be equated with torture as a regular institution.[11]

Of all the famous men of that period the one who became most interested in Beccaria was Voltaire. He was over seventy then, living in Ferney, on Lake Geneva. In October 1765 he received Beccaria's book, brought to him by a young Scotsman, James Macdonald, who had just been in Italy. Only the Italian edition was then available, and Voltaire wrote in a letter to a friend: "I begin to read today the Italian book *On Crimes and Punishments.* At first sight it seems good philosophy; the author is a brother." In the following months Voltaire was busy fighting judicial errors that had come to his attention; and then, in June 1766, he was visited by Morellet, who by this time had translated Beccaria's treatise. The two men discussed the book, and Morellet wrote his Italian friend that Voltaire had admired it greatly and held Beccaria in high esteem. Voltaire now realized the necessity of vast reforms in the criminal law as complementary to the fight against fanaticism and intolerance. Shortly after Morellet's visit, the execution in Abbeville of the Chevalier de La Barre, a young man of twenty who had been found guilty of irreverent acts toward a crucifix, convinced Voltaire that fanaticism and intolerance, combined with a faulty criminal system, could lead to terrible results. The sentence against the Chevalier de La Barre was carried out by five executioners who had been sent to Abbeville from Paris. The young man had been sentenced to have his tongue pulled out, then to have his head cut off and his body burnt to ashes. The arbitrariness of the procedure and the cruelty of the punishment explain why this event was the emotional jolt that made Voltaire decidedly receptive to Beccaria's demand for a complete reform of criminal law. Within a month Voltaire wrote a pamphlet on the Abbeville trial and soon after

---

11. The Italian scholar, Venturi, has doubts about the authenticity of Diderot's comments on Beccaria's treatise and does not exclude the possibility that they might be the work of Jean-François Marmontel, a French writer friend of Morellet. However, it is a fact that Morellet himself, who was in possession of the notes at the time of their first publication, attributed them to Diderot (see Beccaria, *Dei delitti e delle pene,* ed. Venturi, p. 398n).

a *Commentary* on Beccaria's book. Although they were published anonymously, there is no doubt about the authorship of these publications. In his *Commentary* Voltaire endorsed almost all of Beccaria's principles, adding to many of the book's chapters facts and anecdotes as examples of faults and contradictions in the existing penal system. But, like Diderot, Voltaire also unfortunately saw some usefulness in torture as a means of discovering accomplices of avowed criminals; and he refused to condemn capital punishment in principle, simply suggesting that death penalties should be replaced as much as possible by condemnations to forced labor.

This *Commentary* did not represent Voltaire at his best, but its importance was due to the fact that the most popular writer of the century was thereby giving his endorsement to Beccaria's ideas and stressing the urgency of penal reforms. Voltaire's *Commentary* was soon translated into several languages and was added to Beccaria's text in many editions.

Voltaire's writing of the *Commentary* started a relationship between the two men characterized by mutual admiration and the friendliest feelings. Beccaria had instructed his bookseller, Chirol of Geneva, to send him all of Voltaire's publications as soon as they appeared, and there still exist copies of Voltaire's books with Beccaria's marginal notes. Voltaire, on his part, praised Beccaria at every turn, calling him "a beneficent genius whose excellent book has educated Europe." Other admiring references are to be found in many of Voltaire's pamphlets. In July 1766 he wrote to the Prince de Ligne: "Italy is worthy of a visit, not only for her statues and music, as some years ago, but in order to meet thoughtful men who fight against fanaticism and superstition."

In spite of Voltaire's desire to see Beccaria, the two men never met. Although Beccaria planned a trip to Ferney in 1767, he never made it, probably on account of his reluctance to travel, especially after his trip to Paris of which we will soon talk. It is a pity that few letters have been preserved of those exchanged by the two men. One of Voltaire's, dated May 30, 1768, ends with the words: "Why couldn't I have the honor of seeing you, of embracing you and, may I say, of crying with you! At least I have the consolation of telling you how much I esteem you, and how much I love and respect you." It was a touching homage of the seventy-four year old Voltaire to the young Milanese.[12]

---

12. For more details on Voltaire's writings on penal problems in that period see Maestro, pp. 73–99.

4

Il Caffè; The Trip
to Paris

In the already mentioned letter to Morellet of January 26, 1766, Beccaria spoke of a newspaper that he and his friends were publishing in Milan, taking as their model the English *Spectator*. This newspaper, founded by the two Verri brothers together with Beccaria and other members of the group, was called *Il Caffè;* and it is true that the thought of starting a periodical came to them from Addison's *Spectator*. The model was indeed followed fairly closely, even in the idea that the articles were the result of discussions and conversations at the tables of a coffeehouse (hence the name of the paper).

Il Caffè was published regularly for two years, from June 1764 to June 1766, with one issue every ten days. Two subjects were avoided: religion and politics. To be exact, some articles did touch on political problems, but nothing was ever printed that might displease the established authority. The area left open to discussion was, of course, a wide one and the writers of *Il Caffè* dealt, often seriously but sometimes in a light vein, with problems in such disparate fields as literature, language, art, science, law, economics, fashion. Despite the interesting and stimulating articles, the number of readers remained always rather small, sadly reflecting the lack of cultural aspirations in the majority of the Italian public. As Pietro Verri would later lament, a modest subsidy from the government would have enabled *Il Caffè* to continue its publication for a long time, thus contributing to the intellectual education of the people. No help came from the authorities, however, and the life of *Il Caffè* was a short one. In the seventy-four issues that were published appeared numerous excellent articles that can be read today with great pleasure: many of them by Pietro and Alessandro Verri, and several by Beccaria, Frisi, Longo, and Lambertenghi. Beccaria wrote a total of seven articles, a small number if we consider that when the newspaper was founded Beccaria had already finished his treatise *On Crimes and Punishments* and was therefore free from other duties. But that was an exciting period in Beccaria's life. His book published, he was then facing the new experience of sudden and widespread fame. At the same time his young wife, still only twenty years old, was expecting a second child, the little Maria, born in 1766. His first daughter, Giulia, was four years old. Cesare's relationship with his father was now fairly normal. There was, to be sure, a divergence of views and temperament between them, but they lived together without too much trouble in the family house on Via Brera, and in summer they all spent some time at the country estate of Gessate, not far from the city.

The seven articles that Beccaria wrote for *Il Caffè* dealt with a variety of subjects, none of them, strangely enough, having anything to do with legal matters. This diversity showed how wide the range of Beccaria's interests was and how keen his mind was in different fields.[1]

The first article, "Faro," is an extract from an essay by Montmort on the statistical probabilities of winning in this card game. However, the mathematical talent of Beccaria is more evident in another article entitled "Analytical Essay on Smuggling Operations," an interesting attempt to express in a mathematical form the limits of convenience of smuggling operations in the face of the risks involved, the value of the merchandise, and the duty imposed on it. This study, whatever

---

1. These are the Italian titles of the seven articles Beccaria wrote for *Il Caffè:* "Il Faraone," "Tentativo analitico su i contrabbandi," "Risposta alla rinunzia," "Frammento sullo stile," "De' fogli periodici," "I piaceri dell'immaginazione," "Frammento sugli odori." All of Beccaria's articles in *Il Caffè* were signed *C.,* except for the "Essay on Odors," which was signed *A.;* concerning the authorship of these articles see Beccaria, *Opere,* ed. Romagnoli, vol. 1, pp. 139–40.

its practical scope, drew widespread interest as an application of mathematics to a specific economic subject. In fact, as pointed out later by the American economist Irving Fisher, this essay was one of the first mathematical analyses of an economic problem.[2]

In two other articles Beccaria took up linguistic problems. One was a brief and polemical essay in which he derided the obsolete literary forms upheld by the academicians and advocated, instead, a freer style, more closely related to the living language. The second article, entitled "Fragment on Style," was a serious analysis of expressions and words in the evolution of languages. As we will see, the theories of this study were developed later by Beccaria in a separate work on the nature of style, published in 1770.

In "The Periodicals" Beccaria examined the function of newspapers in a society. The inexpensive and easily acquired periodical publications, says Beccaria, have a function that books cannot fill. Books, he says, are often looked upon with suspicion by the less cultivated people; but these same people will not be against reading an unpretentious magazine and they will treat it as they would a friend who has something to tell them. Moreover, in Beccaria's opinion, magazines may appeal much more than books to women who, he says, often find books too heavy for their delicate taste. Beccaria then says that culture may be made accessible to a larger public through newspapers and magazines, and he expresses the hope that *Il Caffè* will contribute to this trend. Of course, Beccaria refers to periodical publications of high moral and literary qualities, as shown by the following words with which he concludes his article:

> We have tried to be useful to our readers by making our own newspaper varied and pleasant. . . . We will be happy if with our articles we will make one good citizen for the country, one good husband or son in a family, or if we will be able to attract some young man to the still unfamiliar field of science. . . . We will be happy if we receive praise for our work and we will do our best to really deserve it.

The remaining two articles, "Pleasures of the Imagination" and the "Essay on Odors," give us further insight into Beccaria's character,

---

2. Irving Fisher, born at Saugerties, N.Y., in 1867, mentioned Beccaria's essay on smuggling operations in the bibliography of the English translation of Cournot's *Recherches sur les principes mathématiques de la théorie des richesses* (1897). Fisher taught mathematics and political economy at Yale University; he wrote *Mathematical Investigations in the Theory of Value and Prices* (1892).

as we follow him in his thoughts on human behavior and in his flights in the realm of fantasy. The essay "Pleasures of the Imagination" undoubtedly was inspired by Mark Akenside's poem of the same title,[3] but Beccaria's version of the subject is quite a personal one, as shown by the following excerpts:

> Wise men know how brief and scarce the pleasures are that come to them in life; but through imagination these pleasures can be lengthened and made more attractive. . . . Men strive and hurt and kill each other in order to reach the few physical pleasures that are spread here and there in the desert of human life. But the pleasures of the imagination can be acquired peacefully, without any danger: they are all ours and they do not arouse any envy, since the majority of people do not know and do not appreciate them. These pleasures may not make the soul inordinately happy, but they give it a serene joy, free from tension, from envy or malice; and they do not push continually those who possess them from hope to fear and from fear to hope.

We know that Beccaria was far from disdaining pleasures which were not imaginary, and his plumpness was certainly a consequence of his love for good food and good wine. Here he justifies the need for such pleasures:

> People who are able to have imaginary pleasures do not refuse from time to time to have some honest physical ones. They need them, after all, in order to nourish the imagination, to get, so to speak, the raw material that they will be able then to mold and tint in many shapes and colors.

Beccaria then tells the reader that it is better to have many small desires rather than compelling and passionate ones. In overly emotional situations, he says, the imagination may become a tyrant instead of a friend and may lead one to unhappiness and insanity. At this point Beccaria gives the reader his prescription for a pleasant life in which serenity and a moderate happiness are the primary objects:

> Do not try to live too fast or too intensely; be as much as possible a spectator of men and do not imitate those who run blindly into

---

3. Mark Akenside (1721–70): his poem *Pleasures of the Imagination,* influenced by Addison's essays, appeared in 1744 in London, and an Italian translation was published in 1763.

each other without knowing where they go. Do what good you can to them, but stay aside and keep at a distance, so that you will not be carried away and drawn into their vortex. . . . If you want to be left in peace, however, you must be at peace with yourself. Do not commit any crime, and be just with all the beings that surround you. Remember that even the smallest creatures, crushed by arrogant and cruel man, are endowed with a little ray of life. If you are wicked and unfair, remorse and uneasiness will be in your blood: uncertainty and fear will then push you, against your will, toward the turmoil and violence of human affairs.

Some of Beccaria's critics commented on this passage and seemed somewhat disturbed by his detached attitude toward his fellowmen and by his cautioning his readers against becoming too impassioned or too involved in human affairs. It seems, however, that Beccaria was addressing his advice also to himself, since he had failed to follow it in many instances.

The essay ends with a poetical counsel by Beccaria to his contemporaries which seems appropriate in any epoch:

Be a friend of blessed solitude, leave frequently the oppressive cities and go out to enjoy free nature, the oldest temple of the gods. Let the mountains echo your songs, let the roaring waves of the sea accompany your hymns. There you will meditate and see some important links of the eternal chain; there you will feel the smallness of our systems and enterprises. You will find everywhere the destructive traces of man, but everywhere you will see how wise nature repairs what man spoils or ruins; because man can alter, but cannot extinguish that essence of life which is a fundamental part of nature.

Of course, in the eighteenth century Beccaria could not foresee the dangers to which nature would be exposed in later times and the degree to which the destructive power of man would grow.

The last of Beccaria's articles in *Il Caffè* is entitled "Essay on Odors." It is an amusing study of the most neglected of our five senses, and a few excerpts from this article will give an idea of Beccaria's approach to this subject:

There is a close relationship between odors and flavors, and these two senses are friendly and faithful to each other. What seems bad to the sense of smell is almost always unpleasant to the palate, and what hurts the palate is rarely liked by the nose. I would think that whatever hurts both is also bad for our health, but doctors and phar-

macists tell me that it is not so. Without their authority I would be
sure that what has a bad effect on the nose and the mouth would be
equally obnoxious to the stomach. . . . Almost nothing has been done
so far for the nose; instead, a lot has been done for the mouth. We
started with the simplest foods, offered by nature; we then had foods
cooked in a simple way, and little by little we have arrived at the
most refined and complicated dishes of the French cuisine. But in
the field of odors we haven't made the slightest progress. Wealth usually gives birth to new needs and new pleasures, but there is not yet
a kitchen of the nose. . . . I think, however, that there could be as
many combinations of odors as there are of foods. I may imagine
living in a more refined century and seeing in the houses of rich
people two cooks, one for the nose and the other for the mouth, and
I would attend odorous banquets where the daintiest dishes of per-
fumes would be served. . . . The dry odors would be symmetrically
placed in little gold and silver cases, while the liquid odors would be
served, as if they were drinks, in crystal phials. There would be warm
odors and cold odors. In the days dedicated to fast and abstinence
there should be a prohibition of voluptuous and sweet odors, only
the chaste and bland should be permitted. The strongest odors would
have a place similar to that of liquors because some of them, the
odor of tobacco for example, bring a momentary euphoria, even
intoxication. It will be time then for a new Anachreon to sing the
praises of inebriating odors, and for a new Mohammed to prohibit
their use.

Beccaria concludes his article on odors by saying that in order to
perfect the neglected sense of smell he has devised a machine made
in the shape of a binocular, which from one side would approach and
enlarge the good odors, and from the other side would push away and
make smaller the bad ones. "I think," says Beccaria, "that this
machine will be used more frequently from the side that pushes away:
just the opposite of what usually happens with the binoculars with
which one looks at things."

Il Caffè continued to be published until June 1766, but even before
the end some of its writers began to leave or to be less active in it. In
fact, less idealistic men would have stopped earlier the publication
of a newspaper that was a financial liability. At any rate, Pietro Verri
had been appointed a member of the Supreme Economic Council of
Milan and now had little time for other work; Alfonso Longo had left
for Rome, and Paolo Frisi was now in Paris. Of the old Accademia
dei Pugni only the name remained, and the last blow came when
Beccaria was able finally to accept the invitation of the French group

of writers and to start on his trip to Paris. The invitation had been extended not only to Beccaria, but also to Pietro Verri; but Pietro was now a government official and could not leave Milan for a prolonged absence. He also may have been a little too proud to go with Beccaria as a less famous man than his former protégé. For these reasons, Pietro Verri thought that his brother Alessandro, a little younger than Beccaria, was the man to go to Paris. And when Beccaria finally said that he was ready for the trip it was agreed, to everybody's satisfaction, that Alessandro would accompany him.

The Trip to Paris

On January 26, 1766, Beccaria had written to his friend and translator Morellet, who had invited him to Paris in the name of all the French writers: "I would rush to Paris if I had the means to do it. . . . I hope that the situation will change. . . ." The situation did change when Beccaria's father became convinced that it would be useful for Cesare's future if he made the trip to Paris and became acquainted with the French intellectual leaders. Plans were made for a six-month absence, and Beccaria's father, having little cash available, went so far as to borrow a substantial amount of money for his son's expensive trip. Equally generous was Alessandro Verri's father, and the two friends left Milan for Paris on October 2, 1766.

It was the first time Beccaria had left Milan for a prolonged trip. A short note written to Pietro Verri a few hours before leaving shows how difficult and painful this departure was for him, and the letters that Beccaria would soon write to his wife confirmed that the pleasure of the trip was from the very beginning somewhat spoiled by his homesickness.

The distance of five or six hundred miles from Milan to Paris was covered, rather leisurely, in about two weeks, and Cesare wrote to his wife from almost every city or town where the coach stopped. His letters are interesting not only for his candid observations and comments about the trip, but for the light they throw on Beccaria's intimate feelings. They also give an idea of what it meant to travel in the eighteenth century.[4] On the same day as his departure Beccaria wrote

---

4. For the full text of Beccaria's letters from his trip to Paris see Beccaria, *Opere,* ed. Romagnoli, vol. 2, pp. 872–92. For Teresa's letters to Beccaria see Vianello, pp. 41–45; for the letters of the Verri brothers see Casati, vol. 1, pp. 195 ff.

to his wife from Novara, the first stopping place on the long trip:

My dear spouse and friend:

My heart knows how much I love you, and Alessandro knows it also. I will not talk of my melancholy in order not to increase yours. I will always love you and I swear that in six months, in exactly 182 days, I will be back in Milan and will be in your arms. Whatever happens, you will always find in me a true friend and a good husband.

Now some pleasant news. We had lunch in Buffalora and were well treated with a very good wine which is a much better comforter than any philosophy; I drank several glasses in order to chase away bad thoughts. Our coachman, Celestino, is a good man, better than any other Milanese coachman, past, present, or future; he goes at a good pace, is good-natured and well-behaved, and does not have some of those Milanese traits that are so unpleasant.

In the afternoon the sun, which is going toward the west, like us, was rather annoying, but now we have recovered and we are in Novara, which is to Milan what Milan is to Paris. This town will be good for my old age, I will come to live here in order to atone for my sins.

Our trip up to now is just a walk. I have no worries, since the hard work is done by the horses and not by us. Alessandrino is very gay and in order to cheer me up he tries not to show that he misses his brother. I will be glad to know that you are happy and serene. Think of how useful this trip may be for both of us, also that my absence will not be long, my dear and lovely spouse.

The next day, October 3, from Vercelli:

My very dear spouse:

We have arrived safely in Vercelli, where we are having dinner with other guests at a round table, something new for us. Vercelli is a very beautiful city, a commercial center, neat and civilized, like none that we have seen so far. There are two magnificent churches, one of Gothic architecture with towers and spires, very attractive; the other is in the Romanesque style with a splendid vestibule. There is nothing similar in our city. Clocks here are already on French time. The city is divided in parishes and their names are written at all street corners, very convenient for travelers. The main square is very beautiful, and I saw there an anemoscope, a device which shows the direction of the wind. All the people here are very kind; there is

---

Baron Paul-Henri d'Holbach (1723–89), mentioned in some of Beccaria's letters from Paris, was a friend of many writers and scholars, and his house became a meeting place for the Parisian intellectual élite. Beccaria was a frequent guest there during his days in Paris.

none of the stupidity and arrogance of Novara. These are the most important events; we are always extremely pleased with our coachman.

I was very unhappy yesterday, being far from you. I almost wanted to go back, and I would have done it if I hadn't been afraid of doing something foolish.

From Turin, capital of Piedmont, the next day, October 4:

I have arrived here, always very pleased with the good manners and cleanliness of our coachman Celestino. The new Turin is really surprising, all streets regularly laid out, all the houses placed at right angles, of the same height and similar palatial architecture . . . and there are majestic squares and a royal palace worthy of the greatest monarch. . . . We went to the comic opera, very poor performance in a small but very neat theater. Excellent treatment in the hotel. . . . My dearest, I think of you every day and I am overcome by sorrowful thoughts when I realize that I am far from you. But I will return soon; this separation has made me feel how dear you are to me.

From Aiguebelle, October 7:

We have crossed the Alps at Mont-Cenis with a beautiful day and without discomfort, since I was well protected against the cold. . . . The last two days I have felt so depressed being far from you that I was ready to go back if I hadn't thought of how ridiculous my act would have been judged for the rest of my life. I didn't know that I loved you so much; you are my happiness. I will certainly return earlier if this depression continues. . . . Give my regards to my father and my mother, greetings to my brothers. Take care of yourself, my love, I will soon write you again.

From Chambéry, October 8:

Only a short note—we just arrived here and I haven't seen the town yet. . . . My depression continues; I will be back in March at the latest. . . . Love me, greetings to everybody.

From Lyons, October 12:

My dear and adorable spouse:

No one must read this letter except my wife.

We arrived in Lyons last night; it is a beautiful city. We went to the theater to see a performance of *Tancrède*. The actor who played

Tancred was even better than Prevost who, you will remember, had that role in Milan. . . . My soul, my dearest, I still haven't received any news from you and I feel very depressed. . . . I am sorry I ever left Milan; it will be difficult for me to stay away even a month or two. If I will not be able to stay at all, I will give the excuse of my health in order to return in an honorable manner. I tell you this, so that you may start saying at home that this air is not good for me. . . . I would like to do all this in the neatest way possible. . . . I think I will see you soon because I am afraid there is no other remedy for my sadness. . . . Greetings to everyone and, above all, two kisses to my dear little daughters, especially to Giulietta who is old enough to understand.

Finally, on October 19, the first letter from Paris:

At last I arrived last night in Paris, very tired from the trip. The city is immense; the number of people, the beauty of the streets, everything is very impressive.

I have seen Frisi, D'Alembert, Morellet, Diderot, and Baron d'Holbach at whose house I had lunch today. You have no idea of the reception, the courtesies, the praises, the demonstrations of friendship and esteem that they all had for me and my friend Alessandro. I am particularly fond of Diderot, d'Hólbach and D'Alembert. D'Alembert is a superior man who at the same time is very simple in his manners. Diderot is always friendly and enthusiastic. I don't miss anything except you, my dear. Everybody tries to please me, and these people are the greatest men of Europe; they are all glad to listen to me, no one shows the slightest air of superiority. I will write you more details later. . . . I am staying in a nice little apartment in the center of the city, near all the people we know. Helvétius and Buffon are still in the country. Morellet is always very kind and thoughtful, a real friend who tries to please us in everything. Remember that I love you tenderly, that to Paris and its attractions I prefer my dear wife, my family, and my friends in Milan, but you above all. This is the truth, my joy, you know that I never lie.

Beccaria was undoubtedly much more upset by the separation from his wife than she was by his being far from her. She was a lively woman, still very young, who liked company and distractions, and could not take her husband's temporary absence too tragically. Beccaria's father told Pietro Verri that on the day of the separation he had found her in tears and was trying to console her, saying that Cesare had left for a good reason and that he would come back soon. To this she answered: "I know all this, I am crying because I will not be able to see Paris."

Perhaps Beccaria was jealous of his pretty wife, knowing that she was admired by numerous young men. Her own letters contain many affectionate expressions, but, despite some dramatic words, they do not convey a feeling of too much unhappiness. She wrote on October 11: "My dear Chesino, please, please write me at every opportunity; even one day of delay makes me desperate and I think I may die." Chesino was short for Marchesino, little Marchese. Beccaria sometimes also called his wife Chesina.

Two days later, on October 13, Teresa wrote that Bartolomeo Calderara, a good friend of the Beccarias, had invited her to one of his villas on Lake Como. Calderara was a handsome and rich young man who was very fond of the Beccarias and often stayed at their house. On his part, he frequently invited the Beccarias to one or another of his country places, and now that Cesare was away only Teresa was left as a possible guest. She wrote to her husband: "I will go to Calderara's villa on the lake for a few days in order to overcome, if possible, the melancholy that oppresses me. Here in the house, now that your sister has come, they are all around her and they didn't even tell me that they were going to Gessate. . . . Believe me, my dearest, I couldn't be more unhappy."

Later she wrote:

> I have been at Ello and Domaso, on Lake Como, and as far as Grigioni; now I am for a day in Milan and then I will go to Pizzighettone and Turano. But I tell you, my sweet, that nothing amuses me, everything makes me sad. Calderara makes fun of me and I cry, and I am patient because he has also good qualities. Dear Chesino, do not write anything about this because Calderara wants to see all your letters and I don't want to make a fool of myself. Please remember this; I told it to you because I tell you everything that I have in my heart.

We may well imagine that Beccaria was far from happy to learn that Calderara read the letters he wrote to Teresa. And it seems strange that in Teresa's letters there was never a word about the daughters, who presumably stayed in Milan with their grandparents when she left the city.

On October 25, exactly a week after his arrival in Paris, Beccaria wrote to his wife that he was more than ever determined to return to Milan as soon as possible:

I have finally received your letter of the 11th. . . . I will tell you very confidentially that my health is good, but you must say the opposite, so that I have a good excuse for leaving. . . . If I could have you come here I would, but this is impossible because it would cost too much. Therefore I am returning to Milan; please help me in this decision. . . . Here I am in the middle of all the most flattering praises and adorations, considered as the friend and equal of the greatest men of Europe, admired and invited by everyone for lunch and dinner in this great capital, going every day to one of the three great theaters, and one of them, the Comédie Française, has the most interesting spectacles in the world; and yet I am sad and unhappy because I am far from you. . . . To my parents I am writing about my health, not as it is, but as it is useful for my purpose. It is hard for me to lie and pretend, but there is no other way; and in this case I am doing something good for myself without harming anyone.

Beccaria's next letter contained a curious piece of news. Some travelers who had been in the southernmost region of South America, called Patagonia, had come back to France with the information that the inhabitants of that land were nine or ten feet tall. Everyone in Paris was talking about this discovery and Beccaria wrote about it to Teresa, saying that a sea captain had brought with him the clothes and weapons of one of those giants. A theory was put forward that all members of the human species were originally of great stature and that the Patagonians were the only giants left because they had lived isolated and unspoiled by contact with other populations. Apparently, Beccaria was intrigued by this theory, but in the end he did not take it too seriously and never referred to it again. As to the statement that the Patagonians were nine or ten feet tall, this was certainly an exaggerated claim; but it is true that members of an Indian tribe of Patagonia, the Tehuelches, were very tall and some individuals may have reached an exceptional height.

The two Verri brothers were unhappy about Beccaria's lack of enthusiasm regarding the trip and about his impulses to return to Milan as soon as possible. From Lyons Beccaria already had written to Pietro that he was sorry he had ever decided to leave Milan, that he was thinking only of his wife, his daughters and his friends, that he didn't know what to do. And from Paris Alessandro described to Pietro how painful the trip had been, how unhappy Beccaria had been all the time, how difficult it had been for Alessandro to convince Beccaria of the foolishness of his attitude: "I thought at moments that he would lose his mind . . . he was absolutely sure that his wife would die. . . . I will never travel again with men who have too much imagination." Also, with some bitterness, he declared: "Here in Paris Beccaria is received with adoration, I am only a satellite. . . . I suppose that this is how it should be, I am not envious."

Pietro Verri tried to dissuade Beccaria from leaving Paris prematurely and wrote him a long letter on October 26 in which he was rather stern toward his old friend:

> Your intention, as described in your letter, has saddened me very much. . . . Some people will ascribe your hurried return to an infantile weakness, and even the most reasonable persons will say that you can rise to a high level with the pen and that you sink to a very low one when you stop writing. . . . I am saying this only because I feel the fear of your shame, the fear that you will be despised for the rest of your life. . . . Your wife is in good health and if she were in Paris instead of you she would not have your worries; your daughters are well also and do not need you. Your good father would certainly be sorry if the money he gave you served not to bring praise for you and help to find you a good position, but to make you a laughing-stock and to show that you don't know how to behave in life. . . . I tell you all this as a friend who knows that your good qualities more than compensate for your faults . . . a friend who asks you to have some pity on yourself and on your reputation.

Pietro Verri went so far as to ask Teresa to write her husband to think again before coming back, and she in fact wrote: "Perhaps some people will say that you were not well received in Paris if you come back now; and also I think that if you stay longer you may find something good for your career." But Beccaria remained unmoved and on November 15 he told Pietro that his decision was indeed final. Answering Pietro's letter he wrote:

> You speak to me with your heart and the sincerity of your friendship, and therefore, far from feeling hurt, I am grateful to you for what you wrote, except for a few sentences that displeased me. . . . All your reasons are futile in the present circumstances; Alessandro had already put them forward with equal conviction . . . and on account of them I dragged myself to Paris, like a wretch on his way to be executed, and I swallowed my sadness and my pain, and tried everything in order to get over this state of mind; it was all useless, as Alessandro already wrote you.

Anyhow, I had planned to be absent for four or five months. Now it will be only two; but can't a traveler find many reasons for shortening his trip? Health, business, family affairs, and so on. If my friends and my family are on my side, all the gossip will be put to rest. Years ago I didn't hesitate to shock the whole of Milan by going ahead with the marriage I wanted, and I had nothing to my credit at that time. . . . And now, when I have in my hand the approving votes of all Europe, should I be afraid of returning two months before I had planned to my city and my family, and should I care about what the Milanese will think of me? Don't be worried about my reputation. In my heart there is nothing that is not good and honest; any small damage will be repaired, and the Milanese will be nice and again have a good opinion of me. . . .

Dear friend, I will soon be thirty years old; let me be as I am, let me follow my career in peace according to my feelings, my character, my needs. . . . In any case, my short visit to Paris has been profitable, I have made many useful and important friendships, I have sowed my future happiness. I used well the money given to me by my father, part of which I haven't spent. It is true, this money was not given to me in order to make me ridiculous, but it was not given to make me unhappy either. . . .

One thing I ask of your friendship, that you prepare my father for this return, so as to spare me useless reproaches and domestic troubles. . . . You will always be my friend and I want to be always yours.

In spite of this last statement Beccaria's friendship with the Verris had already weakened, and, as we will see, their relationship was soon to deteriorate further. At the beginning of December Beccaria was ready to start on his trip back. He took leave of his French friends and of Alessandro Verri (who was to stay a while longer in Paris before going to London and later to Rome where he finally settled), and on December 12, 1766, Beccaria was back in Milan. He had been away about ten weeks, six of which he had spent in Paris.

5

The Hostility of
the Verris;
The Teaching Career

 T HE Italian critics have given various interpretations to Beccaria's behavior during his French trip. Cesare Cantù, one of the first writers to study Beccaria's life and his contribution to the improvement of penal laws, does not see anything very strange in his conduct. He sees in Beccaria a man with an independent mind, more interested in the simple pleasures of family life than in the applause of the greatest men of Europe; and Beccaria's desire to be with his wife is viewed as a natural feeling of two young married people who are still deeply in love. Cantù is convinced that Beccaria's feelings for his wife were reciprocated by her love for him, and he dismisses the idea that there were reasons for Beccaria to be jealous of her. Another critic, R. Mondolfo, gives a simple explanation of Beccaria's behavior: "His friend Longo was right; when they asked him why Beccaria was reluctant to go to Paris where so many satisfactions for his pride were waiting for him, he answered that Beccaria had the most pleasant of reasons for his reluctance: a beautiful wife."

But not all comments are equally charitable. C.A. Vianello describes Beccaria as a rather unsteady person, a prey to morbid impulses, one whose stubborn resolutions are typical of people without real willpower; and Vianello's somewhat sarcastic remarks about Beccaria's wife are meant to imply that her faithfulness was not above suspicion. An even more extreme view is held by the criminologist Cesare Lombroso, who in the second half of the nineteenth century advanced the theory that genius is always accompanied by some sort of insanity and is produced in a person only at the expense of some other faculties. Lombroso cites the examples of many great men as proof of his theory and, basing his findings about Beccaria mostly on his behavior during the Parisian trip, argues that we have here the example of a brilliant man who is at the same time infantile and subject to hysterics and hallucinations.

Discarding Lombroso's terminology and the conclusions based on gossip or on biased accounts, the fact remains that Beccaria's conduct during the Parisian trip was peculiar and immature. We should accept this fact and acknowledge that at times Beccaria was, indeed, oversensitive and showed unjustified fears and emotions. These were traits of his character, part of his whole person; without them he would have been another man. It seems fair, therefore, to accept Beccaria as he was, remembering that he himself had asked his friends to let him live according to his feelings, his character, and his needs.

The Verris' Change in Attitude

Despite Beccaria's persistent homesickness, the six weeks that he spent in Paris had been profitable, as he himself wrote; he did enjoy the great city, the matinées at the theaters, the discussions with French writers. From Alessandro Verri's somewhat sour confession we know that Beccaria was always the star of the parties and apparently did not disappoint the French group that had invited him to Paris. Alessandro confirmed this in several of his letters to his brother, in which we notice a growing hostility toward his companion. Here are some excerpts from Alessandro's letters to Pietro, first from a letter of November 21, 1766, while Beccaria was still in Paris:[1]

> You are right, I shouldn't say anything in public against Beccaria . . . it would only harm me in the eyes of his friends, who are all enthusiastic about him. He seems to all so kind, so good-hearted, and they will consider anything critical of him as a malicious lie. And

---

1. For the letters of the Verri brothers up to the end of December, 1766, see Casati, vol. 1, pp. 292 ff.; after January 1, 1767, Casati, vol. 2, pp. 1 ff.

yet this man who seems so good is full of bitterness, of jealousy, of ingratitude. . . . We go to the theater almost every day; it starts at half past five. Then, at half past eight, after the theater, we usually go to dinner at Baron d'Holbach's house or to a party at Mademoiselle Lespinasse's. Sometime I prefer to go home, and this annoys our friend, who would like me to stay for his convenience, not because he cares if I stay or not. He is perfectly at home in these groups without me, and yet he is angry if I don't want to stay.

In another letter, written from London a few weeks later, on December 29, Alessandro complained that in Paris he had been a victim of Beccaria's literary jealousy. "You may think that this trait in Beccaria is new," wrote Alessandro to Pietro, "but I can assure you that he is indeed jealous of other writers, and of me especially." And Alessandro explained to Pietro how frustrating the situation had been for him:

> Beccaria was interested only in himself, and therefore few people were able to appreciate me. . . . Only Beccaria shone and was listened to, since Beccaria was in fashion in true Parisian style, because there they always go to extremes—all or nothing; and poor Verri was silent in a corner, neglected. After dinner Beccaria was feeling gay, having drunk some glasses of good wine (I know only too well how he likes it!), and couldn't care less about me. . . . He was there, intoxicated by his glory, full of brilliant conversation, determined not to let me open my mouth, talking forever.

A few days later, on January 15, 1767, Alessandro told his brother what poor reasoners and debaters the French writers were: "I saw them every day being left behind by Beccaria's logic; he could reduce to the simplest terms an enormous quantity of words and confused ideas. Neither D'Alembert nor any of the others has Beccaria's precision, nor yours, nor—modestly—mine."

Alessandro's praise comes almost as a surprise, and he soon went back to his disparaging statements. Returning to Paris from London in February of 1767, Alessandro wrote to Pietro that Beccaria had left a dubious reputation in the French capital; but by now we can put very little faith in what Alessandro says. The truth is that the letters sent to Beccaria by his French friends show only respect and affection for him, despite the undoubted attempts of Alessandro to put him in a bad light. A few months after Beccaria's departure Morellet, answering a letter from Beccaria, asked him if he had recovered his peace of mind and expressed the hope that he would continue to enlighten men and work for their well-being and happiness. Baron d'Holbach also wrote to Beccaria in very cordial terms:

> I received your dear letter of January 20 and I was happy seeing that you have not forgotten the poor Parisians whom you cruelly abandoned when they were hoping to enjoy your pleasant company during the whole winter. Be assured that they all hope to be worthy of your friendship and that they admire and love you. . . . These are the feelings of our whole group; all have asked me to be their spokesman and to send you their greetings.

D'Alembert also wrote a friendly letter to Beccaria: "I am very flattered by what you say about my latest work because your appreciation is one which I wish most to deserve. . . . All our mutual friends send you their compliments."

Finally, we quote from the memoirs of Amélie Suard, the wife of the publisher of the *Gazette littéraire de l'Europe,* which had printed an early review of Beccaria's book:

> Not long after my marriage we had supper with the marquis Beccaria. He had published his treatise *On Crimes and Punishments* and the French translation by Morellet was then having the greatest success. . . . The marquis Beccaria must have been quite pleased with the way he was received in Paris. He was made the object of the most enthusiastic praises and marks of esteem and admiration. He was rather small in stature, but he had a face that one could never forget; he had regular features and his eyes, of exceptional beauty, seemed to shine with the flame of genius. He was very proud and at the same time he had the sweetest and most sensitive soul.[2]

From all the above testimony it is quite clear that in Paris Beccaria had not always been in a melancholy mood, but had had moments of great enthusiasm and excitement in the discussions with his French friends. His temperament, it seems, had not changed much from the time of his high school days in Parma, when his teachers had noticed the ease with which his mood changed suddenly for no important reason. It is also clear from these accounts that the French writers had enjoyed Beccaria's visit, that they had given him the opportunity

---

2. See Venturi, *Settecento riformatore—Da Muratori a Beccaria,* p. 744n (quoting from Amélie P. Suard, *Essais de mémoires sur M. Suard,* Paris: Didot, 1820).

to shine in their conversations, that they had not been particularly disturbed by his hurried departure, and that—contrary to Alessandro Verri's assertion—there was nothing dubious about the reputation which Beccaria had left in Paris. Furthermore, the French writers maintained the friendliest relations with Beccaria for several years, as proved by their correspondence.[3]

The fear expressed by the Verris that Beccaria's good name in Milan would be spoiled by his shortened sojourn in Paris turned out also to be unfounded. Pietro Verri gave a rather unconvincing account to his brother of the Milanese reaction. According to Pietro, some people ascribed Beccaria's early return to his disappointment at not being well received in Paris, others thought he had quarrelled with Alessandro, and still others were convinced that Beccaria had returned earlier because he had spent all his money on books. The fact is that, besides these vague statements by Pietro Verri, we have no indication at all that Beccaria had lost any prestige among the Milanese, who apparently did not care whether Beccaria had returned from Paris a little earlier or a little later than previously announced. As a matter of fact, Beccaria's good standing with the authorities was soon to be concretely demonstrated.

While Alessandro Verri had been the first to show hostility toward Beccaria, partly because of differences in their temperaments and partly because Alessandro had resented the secondary position in which he had found himself in Paris, it was Pietro who soon became even more vindictive and implacable toward his old friend. In every letter to his brother, Pietro now showed feelings of increasing enmity toward Beccaria which at first are not easily explained. We should remember at this point that although Alessandro was only twenty-six at the time—three years younger than Beccaria—Pietro was a much more mature man, ten years older than Beccaria. Perhaps, at least at the start, a protective feeling toward his younger brother had contributed to Pietro's attitude, as can be seen from a letter written to Alessandro when he and Beccaria were still in Paris: "What can I say to you? I see from your letter that you are completely right and Beccaria is completely wrong; your heart is ulcerated by his conduct, and so is mine."

---

3. For the letters written to Beccaria by his French friends after his trip to Paris see Landry, pp. 141 ff.

After Beccaria's return to Milan Pietro wrote: "Beccaria arrived yesterday, received with the greatest sweetness by his dear spouse. . . . I saw him today and he told me frankly that nobody is dearer to him than his wife. . . . He didn't say a word to show that anyone in Paris knows of my existence. . . . You see that he treats me as he treated you." And a few days later: "There are more and more reasons for the coolness in my friendship with Beccaria. . . . He will try to come back to me once the Parisian aura has evaporated, but the pure flame that I had for his glory will not be there and he will not have my heart anymore. . . . Europe has declared that he is greater than I; my own conscience says the opposite."

These words seem to indicate the real reasons for Pietro's growing bitterness; and yet he tries to find for it some worthier motive, as shown by the following letter full of contradictions:

> I can't have any more friendship for Beccaria. I really have no animosity toward him, nor can I reproach him for anything. He never lied to me, he never was disrespectful toward me. It was not his fault if I continued to think that he was capable of true friendship. He is not able to deceive or simulate, that would be too tiring for him; he enjoys the pleasures that men give him, and since the greatest pleasures come from his friends, he enjoys friendship very much. . . . Now he wants to enjoy his good luck and the superiority that the public has given him over his friends; his friends resent his attitude, this resentment is painful to Beccaria, and therefore he avoids his friends.

Clearly, Pietro was trying to find an honorable reason for his decision to break with Beccaria. In another letter, soon after, he wrote:

> I saw Carli and Countess Somaglia, and they both think that Beccaria has changed very much since his return, that he now smiles with an air of superiority and gives the impression that he is there to protect the unhappy human species. . . . As long as Beccaria needed a friend he found it in me; now his needs have changed, and he is looking for satellites and protégés. . . . He has had his little luck with his book, but he forgets that men are capricious and in a few years he may not have all this admiration; and he forgets that if we two really wanted it, we could destroy his reputation. . . . In a month I could find in Montesquieu, in Voltaire and in Grevius many passages similar to his, so that he would look like a plagiarist. I will not do this, but I am satisfied that I could do it if I wanted to.

How fortunate for Pietro's own good name that he did not! These remarks from Pietro to Alessandro were answered by similar ones from Alessandro, and they were often accompanied by epithets such as rascal, animal, clown, or worse. It became an obsession that lasted for many years and filled a large part of the correspondence of the two brothers, Pietro writing from Milan and Alessandro now from Rome.

The interesting fact in all this is that the object of so much attention, of so many outbursts and insults, had no idea that hundreds of invectives against him filled the letters of his former friends. Beccaria was unaware of this, but he knew, of course, that the friendship was over, and he undoubtedly knew of derogatory remarks made about him by the Verris to mutual friends and acquaintances. It is not easy to assess how much influence this hostility had on Beccaria's other friendships, but he undoubtedly was saddened by it, whatever its practical results. Some of his old friends could not understand the reasons for the rupture, finding it difficult to believe that it was the success of Beccaria's book that was the real motive for Pietro Verri's spite. Being apparently unable to confess, even to himself, that this was the reason for his new attitude, Pietro had to construct an image of Beccaria that would justify his hostility toward his old friend. It was hard, however, for those who had known Beccaria to accept Pietro's version of the facts, as shown for example by the following letter of Alfonso Longo, the former collaborator on *Il Caffè,* now living in Rome. In answer to a letter from Pietro he wrote:

> I see from what you have written me that you have almost broken with Beccaria. Since I have known him for a long time, you didn't need to give me any information about his character. I agree with you that he is not always the most sociable and obliging person in the world; that is why you had your little fights and why he had frequent ones with Alessandro. When they left together on their trip I thought that the difference in their temperaments might well produce some hot discussions. . . . But this has nothing to do with your friendship . . . and I am unable to understand how Beccaria can be contemptuous toward you, how he can make you feel the weight of his glory, how he can be ungrateful to you, who have done so much for him, have always encouraged and defended him. Permit me not to believe yet that he is capable of such baseness . . . for, you must admit this yourself, Beccaria has a good and sensitive heart, and this is why you judged him worthy of your friendship. . . . I simply can't believe that Beccaria is capable of such a change. Please tell me that

it isn't so, that your friendship has been renewed; or (what can I say?) explain to me how Beccaria, worthy of esteem for so many reasons, has turned out to be the most ungrateful of men. . . .

Please be assured that I believe what you have written me . . . although I am surprised by what has happened. Since it is so, however, let us forget his faults, let us not consider him any longer an intimate friend, but let us not push our vengeance to the point of hating him. . . . We will talk about all this; in the meantime try to moderate your resentment toward him, even if it is justified.[4]

In this letter Longo certainly tried hard to please Pietro Verri, though refusing to endorse his new attitude toward Beccaria. Unfortunately Longo's plea for a more reasonable approach was not heeded by the two brothers, who developed a real hatred toward their old friend. Beccaria always maintained a dignified silence about this whole affair, partly because the worst attacks launched against him by the two Verris were kept secret in their own private correspondence. He could never know, therefore, what they said and thus could not possibly answer them. It was a vicious circle: Beccaria's silence would make the Verris angrier because their attacks had no effect, so that they had to renew them continually without ever getting any reaction or satisfaction. Only after the death of the three men was the correspondence of the Verris made public, and it did no credit to the two brothers.

As was said before, it is not easy to explain the bitter feelings and the long-lasting hostility of the Verris toward Beccaria, especially the attitude of Pietro, who undoubtedly had had a warm and sincere sympathy for him until his Parisian trip. To be sure, Beccaria was not entirely blameless: he had disappointed his old friend by refusing to listen when he had tried to dissuade him from leaving Paris too soon; it seems also—if one can believe Alessandro's story—that in Paris, when some French friends had mentioned Facchinei's polemical pamphlet, Beccaria was not prompt enough to give credit to the Verris for being the authors of the *Apology* in answer to it. These are small matters, however, which could not have changed Pietro's feelings so completely. Perhaps Pietro's enmity would not have been so intense if he had not been so fond of Beccaria before. Everything considered, we must conclude reluctantly that envy and jealousy must

---

4. For the text of Longo's letter to Pietro Verri see Vianello, pp. 51–56.

have been the prime motives of this hostility. These feelings are not praiseworthy, but they are to be found in many human beings, even in people whose accomplishments we admire.

Appointment to the Palatine School

Until his return from Paris Beccaria had lived mostly on an allowance from his father, but he was not happy about his continued dependence on his parents and had tried earnestly to find a government position in which he could use his best talents. In 1765, after the publication of his treatise *On Crimes and Punishments,* he had decided to send a copy of that book, as well as a copy of his previous essay on the monetary problems in Milan, to Archduke Ferdinand of Austria, who was then the titular governor of Lombardy.[5]

Beccaria had written in an accompanying letter:

> The two little books that I have the honor to present to Your Highness are the fruit of the peace and protection enjoyed by the citizens living under the merciful dominion of Her Majesty [Maria Theresa] and under the fortunate and wise administration of Your Highness. . . . I must confess that to a forensic career I have preferred to dedicate myself to those sciences which tend to regulate the economy of a state. Your Highness will forgive me if I write that I would be very happy if I could put myself and my energies at Her Majesty's service. I think that an honorable citizen may express this desire in the confident expectation of some favorable decision.

Despite the beautiful expressions, nothing came of the letter. And we know that the trip to Paris was undertaken also in the hope of some practical result. Beccaria's father had favored the trip for that very reason, and Teresa had shown in several of her letters that she was eager for Cesare to be financially independent. She had not forgotten how humiliatingly she had been received in the family, and even now her relations with its various members were not always pleasant, especially those with Cesare's sister, Maddalena.

While Beccaria was in Paris something at last began to move, and from quite an unexpected quarter: from the new, modern capital of Russia, St. Petersburgh, where the German-born Catherine the Great

---

5. Ferdinand, Archduke of Austria and Duke of Modena, was governor of Lombardy; he was assisted by a high officer for military matters and by a minister plenipotentiary for civilian affairs (the position held by Count Firmian). See Landry, pp. 219–20.

had ascended the throne a few years before. On November 18, 1766, while Beccaria was still in Paris, a friend of his, Gaspare Angiolini, whose talents as a choreographer were appreciated highly by Catherine, wrote him a letter from Russia in which he referred to the treatise *On Crimes and Punishments.* "I am pleased to tell you," wrote Angiolini, "that our empress has already read your book and that she was touched by the strength with which you have served and sustained the cause of humanity."

Catherine had received the book some time before from D'Alembert, with whom she was in regular correspondence, as she was with Voltaire, Diderot, and other French writers. She was so impressed by Beccaria's book that she decided to summon a commission to Moscow and then to St. Petersburgh for the purpose of compiling a new, complete code of laws; and she herself wrote the *Instructions* for the new code, following—as she explained it—the principles of the Western philosophers, above all Beccaria. It was only logical that, in her desire for reforms, she should call on the Milanese writer as the ideal man to give practical effect to his theories and organize on new bases the criminal system of Russia. The offer came from a representative of Catherine in Milan, Antonio Greppi, who inquired if Beccaria would be interested in such a position and on what terms he would be willing to go to Russia.[6]

As soon as Beccaria arrived in Milan from Paris he was faced with this important decision. His wife was in favor of accepting the Russian offer, which would solve all their financial problems and give them their independence from all their relatives. This time they would not be separated, but would go together to an important capital, where Cesare would be a respected man at the imperial court and in society. All this appealed to romantic Teresa, but Beccaria was not so sure about going to what at that time seemed a distant and unfamiliar

---

6. Antonio Greppi was an indirect representative of Catherine II of Russia; she had given instructions for the offer to Beccaria to a commercial agent of Venice in St. Petersburgh, named Pano Maruzzi, who asked Greppi to get in touch with Beccaria. For more details about this offer see Landry, pp. 142–44n and Vianello, pp. 83–88. For Catherine's efforts to reform the Russian penal system see Maestro, pp. 136–38.

For more details on this subject see Rambaud, *Histoire de la Russie depuis les origines jusqu'à nos jours,* pp. 476 ff.; also *Documents of Catherine the Great— The Correspondence with Voltaire and the Instruction of 1767 in the English Text of 1768,* pp. 215–309.

place. He did not want to refuse the offer, especially if his wife was in favor of it, but he wanted to think it over and asked for the advice of several friends, among them Morellet and D'Alembert in Paris.

Beccaria did not receive much encouragement from his Parisian friends. Morellet wrote:

> I don't understand how you can seriously ask if you should go to Russia. If you had no family and no friends, if you were in a country with a bad climate, I would say: go. But in your situation it would be insane, especially with your character and your anxieties: you would certainly be very unhappy if you were far from your friends, from your country, far from the new books and without contacts with writers and men of letters. You need these things more than anyone else.

D'Alembert was no less forceful:

> Please think well before taking a decision. . . . Remember that if you go to Russia you would give up a very beautiful climate for an ugly country, you would give up freedom for slavery, and you would leave your friends for a princess who is full of merits, it is true, but it is better to have her as a mistress than as a wife."[7]

It is clear that D'Alembert, who himself had refused an offer from Catherine to settle in Russia, did not want to see his Milanese friend sign away his own freedom. Despite these negative reactions, Beccaria was in no hurry to reject the Russian offer and he decided in the meantime to talk to his protector, Count Carlo Firmian, in order to see if there was a possibility of employment in Milan itself. The fact that the empress of Russia had offered him an important position in St. Petersburgh was an ace in Beccaria's hand and he had decided to use it. Firmian wrote to the Austrian chancellor in Vienna, Prince Kaunitz, that Beccaria had received the Russian offer but was in doubt about accepting it before he knew what possibilities there were for him in his own country.[8]

---

7. For the full text of Morellet's and D'Alembert's letters to Beccaria see Landry, pp. 141–46 and 149–50.

8. Prince Kaunitz-Rittberg (1711–94), court and state chancellor since 1753, followed with special interest the affairs of the Low Countries and of Lombardy. Concerning the problems of this Italian province he was assisted by Baron Sperges (1726–91), born in Innsbruck, a learned man, very familiar with the Italian language and culture.

Prince Kaunitz's answer showed that he was quite familiar with Beccaria's work. He asked for some additional information, saying that from his book Beccaria appeared to be a thoughtful man. It may be wise, said Kaunitz, not to let another government take precedence in securing his services. Firmian promptly gave the chancellor the most favorable information as to Beccaria's moral qualities and suggested that perhaps he could be appointed professor of public law at the Palatine School of Higher Learning in Milan. Prince Kaunitz agreed with the proposal, but pointed out that an educational reform involving the Palatine School was then being carried out; it would be necessary, therefore, for Beccaria to wait until this reform was completed.

Being virtually assured of the desired position in Milan, Beccaria decided at last to reject the offer from Catherine II. Almost a year had elapsed since she first had shown an interest in him, and in view of Beccaria's hesitation she had by then asked another legal scholar, the Frenchman Mercier de la Rivière, to come to Russia for the enactment of penal reforms. However, her great project was to be realized only partially. In the following years Catherine did correct some legal abuses and abolished the use of torture. But Mercier de la Rivière, who had accepted Catherine's invitation, was not the right man for the gradual and patient work that was required. A war against Turkey made matters even more difficult. It should be said, however, that if Catherine did not succeed in accomplishing as much as she had desired, this was due partly to the lukewarm response she received from a still backward population.

In any case, Beccaria's Russian adventure was over. In the meantime he was busy writing an essay on style, enlarging and developing the much smaller article that he had written on this subject for *Il Caffè*. His relationship with Pietro Verri, although never completely broken, had become cold and formal. At this time Beccaria became more attached to an old friend, Gian Rinaldo Carli, who in 1765 had been named president of the Supreme Economic Council of Milan, of which Pietro Verri was a member. In the summer of 1768 Beccaria went with his wife to Bagni di Pisa, a resort that had been suggested as the right place for Teresa, whose health in recent months had not been good. After a sojourn at Bagni di Pisa the couple decided to return to Milan by a roundabout way, stopping at Bologna, Ferrara, and Venice. Beccaria wrote from Bagni di Pisa to his friend Carli to thank him for several letters of recommendation which Carli had given him. "If you don't mind," wrote Beccaria, "please let me know of some good lodging in Venice, so that we are not cheated as travelers usually are."

Soon after his return to Milan Beccaria received the good news of his new position. On November 1, 1768, Count Firmian informed Beccaria that the government was entrusting to him the newly established chair of public economy and commerce at the Palatine School. Beccaria was quite pleased that the chair had been founded with him in view. It seemed to him preferable to the teaching of public law that had been suggested earlier.

The Palatine School was one of the two institutes of higher learning in the Milan area, the other being the ancient University of Pavia, where Beccaria had received his degree. The educational reform which had just been completed, while confirming in its importance the Pavia school, had considerably enlarged the scope of the Milanese institution, increasing from six to fourteen the number of its chairs. However, while the Pavia University had complete courses up to the doctoral degree, the Palatine School retained the character of a less formal college with less rigorous requirements.

On November 7, 1768, Beccaria thanked Count Firmian for his intervention and, soon after, he also sent a grateful letter to Prince Kaunitz, who had obtained from Empress Maria Theresa the decree establishing the new chair at the Palatine School. In her decree Maria Theresa wrote that in her willingness always to give her people all possible advantages, one being the promotion of learning, she had decided to establish in Milan a chair of public economy to be entrusted to Cesare Beccaria, "who has acquired with his works a good name among learned men." The imperial decree added that this study would be compulsory for all those who aspired to public positions in the economic and financial fields.[9]

The establishment of a chair of economics was a great event in Italy at that time. Even in England and in France, where the study of economics had been flourishing for some time and the importance of this science had been recognized, regular courses in it were still only

---

9. For details of Maria Theresa's decree and Beccaria's appointment to the chair of public economy at the Palatine School see Cantù, pp. 169–70n. For more information on the Palatine School of Milan see Vianello, pp. 88 ff.; also Visconti, *Le Scuole Palatine di Milano*.

in the developing stage. In Italy the only department of economics which had preceded the one in Milan was the department established in 1754 in Naples, where the instruction had been entrusted to the well-known economist Antonio Genovesi.

The Austrian government, a few months before the final approval of the new chair in Milan, had asked the president of the economic council, Carli, to submit a plan showing how the course should be conducted—it being understood that the classes would be completed in two years. Carli asked Beccaria to draw up this plan himself, and Beccaria wrote it in a short time, following fairly closely a French model; he made clear, however, that his teaching would take into special consideration the position of the empire, and of Lombardy in particular, since many of the students would then be candidates to public offices in the area. Beccaria proposed to divide his two-year course into five parts: (1) general principles and theories of the economic science, (2) agriculture, (3) commerce, (4) industry, (5) finance. After explaining how the five main parts should be subdivided, Beccaria concluded the description of his plan with these words:

> If there is some time left at the end of the course I propose to further give a general view of European trade as a whole. This will help to enlarge the young people's ideas, because a man can never be great if he confines himself to what he sees within the borders of his own country.

Carli presented Beccaria's plan, accompanied by his own approving report, and the Viennese authorities evidently were satisfied, so that the appointment, as we have seen, was confirmed shortly after.

The personal note at the end of Beccaria's plan is indicative of his political outlook. Beccaria was a humanist and it was natural for him to consider mankind as a whole and to see all problems primarily as human problems. His political position was a simple one: he accepted without any question the situation as he had found it and saw nothing wrong in Milan's being under Austrian rule. Although his language and his culture were Italian, he quite naturally thought of himself as an Austrian citizen whose loyalty was due to the Austrian government. The Austrian empire was a multinational state in which the various ethnic groups and languages were generally respected, and under Maria Theresa the Austrian rule in Italy had been in many ways an enlightened one. Although it is true that all the important decisions concerning the Italian provinces were made in Vienna, it must be noted that the department for Italian affairs in the Austrian capital was usually directed by competent officials. The idea of a united and independent Italy developed only in the nineteenth century. In Beccaria's time there were few in Italy who thought along nationalistic lines, and in Milan the majority of the population accepted the reality of the Austrian rule without discussion. That atmosphere may have made it easier for Beccaria to look beyond all borders and to be, in a sense, a citizen of the world.[10]

In the letter of thanks that Beccaria wrote to Count Firmian on November 7, 1768, he promised to follow the schedule of his plan for the future course, as well as any direction he would receive later. He also informed Firmian that, taking into consideration the time needed for adequate preparation, he would be ready for the inaugural address—called in Italian *prolusione*—soon after the Christmas holidays, while the regular lectures could be initiated a few weeks after. His dates were accepted, and on January 9, 1769, the young professor—not yet thirty-one years old—delivered his opening address in the great hall of the Palatine School. This was the beginning of a phase in Beccaria's life in which he would be concerned mostly with economic problems, first as a teacher and a theoretician, and later as a member of the government council where economic problems were to be studied and solved. It is necessary to pause here, however, and speak of Beccaria's writings in the period preceding the start of this new assignment.

---

10. An interest in the national question was shown by Gian Rinaldo Carli: in an article entitled "Della patria degli Italiani" ("The Fatherland of the Italians," published in *Il Caffè*) he expressed the view that there was a common bond among all the inhabitants of the Italian peninsula, whatever their national allegiance. However, not even Carli was advocating a more intimate *political* bond among all the Italians; such a suggestion would have displeased the Austrian authorities and therefore could not have been printed in *Il Caffè*.

6

Research on the Nature of Style

THE book on which Beccaria had been working since his return from Paris was an essay entitled *Ricerche intorno alla natura dello stile.* This subject, the nature of style, had appealed to Beccaria since the time of *Il Caffè,* for which he had written a "Fragment on Style." He had planned then to develop his article into a more serious study and he began to work on the project after his trip to Paris while waiting for a decision about his career. Finally, in 1770, when he was teaching economics at the Palatine School, the book was printed in Milan by the publisher Galeazzi. It was, to be exact, only the first part of his projected book, and Beccaria promised in the introduction that a second part would follow in a short time. He was unable to complete the work, however, and only a chapter of the second part was found after Beccaria's death. This chapter, although not elaborated as originally planned, concludes the whole work and was added to the first part in the Italian edition of the book which was published posthumously in 1809.

This was not an easy book for Beccaria to write, since the work was done while he was occupied with other problems and worried about his future position, and in a way it refutes the widespread legend that Beccaria lacked energy and willpower. To be sure, this opinion was based partly on Beccaria's own confession that indolence was one of his traits; and he mentioned laziness as a reason for not answering letters more promptly. The Verri brothers helped to give credence to this opinion by stating repeatedly that Beccaria needed continual prodding in order to do anything, and it is not surprising that this belief was accepted without too much discussion by all the Italian students of Beccaria, even by those who felt the greatest sympathy and admiration for him.

Was Beccaria really lazy or indolent? And was he so incapable of deciding what he should do? It is true that he was not the most energetic of men nor the most productive of writers. But it is also true that what is viewed as lack of energy sometimes signifies gentleness and modesty; and limited productivity may mean conscientiousness and a determination to think seriously before writing. We know that Beccaria had moments of indecision, that he was sometimes unnecessarily worried and unreasonably timid, but his whole life seems to belie the legend of his indolence and lack of willpower. He undoubtedly knew how to dedicate himself to a task he valued highly, and all through his life he seemed to know fairly clearly what he wanted.

The publication of his *Research on the Nature of Style* is a proof of Beccaria's ability to work hard when he thought he was facing a challenging task. This was a work that required much study and application in a difficult field, and we may say at the outset that Beccaria succeeded only in part in his ambitious goal. Italian critics have given a variety of judgments on this work. To mention two extreme viewpoints, Francesco De Sanctis dismissed it as a useless exercise, while R. Mondolfo considered Beccaria's essay an important contribution to the history of esthetics. More than that, according to Mondolfo, Beccaria would now be regarded as one of the great philosophers of the eighteenth century if he had developed further some of the original ideas that he outlined in his book.[1]

Unfortunately, these ideas were not developed, and the book remained somewhat uneven and incomplete. Imperfect as it is, it reveals, nevertheless, the scope of Beccaria's intellectual gifts which

---

1. See De Sanctis, *Teoria e storia della letteratura,* vol. 2, p. 69, and Beccaria, *Opere scelte,* ed. Mondolfo, pp. xxxi–xli.

enabled him to touch on a variety of subjects, from juridical science and economics to problems of language and literary style.

The essay was dedicated in elegant style by Beccaria to his old friend and protector, Count Firmian: "With the most sincere feelings of gratitude I offer you this work which perhaps will have the sole, although glorious, merit of having your name in the front and of giving the author the hope that he will still have in the future your highly appreciated patronage."

An interesting and appealing idea of unity in man's endeavors and accomplishments is expressed at the outset in the preface:

> It may seem that, since I previously wrote of political matters and of the unhappy condition of criminal procedures, and since I have now received the task of instructing young people in the science that aims at the well-being of men, I have changed my path and neglected my other duties in order to enter the fascinating areas of language and literature. But there is no reason for surprise if we consider that beauty, goodness, and usefulness are closely related to one another and have all one thing in common: the love of happiness. It follows that morality, politics, and the fine arts, which are the sciences of goodness, usefulness, and beauty, are related sciences, having a greater identity of principles than one may imagine. These sciences all have their origin in one first science, the science of man; and we cannot hope to make great and rapid progress in those derivative sciences if we do not first study the fundamental principles of the science of man. This truth will be developed in the proper place, but I wanted to indicate this here in order to justify this work and to show that I have not gone far astray from my other subjects.

The idea that we should look to man as the source of all the facts that special sciences study separately seems to point toward an all-embracing philosophy in which all branches of human knowledge would fall into place. But—despite Beccaria's promise in his preface—this theory is never fully explained and elaborated, and a real doctrine or philosophical system is never really developed. We may say the same of other interesting ideas contained in this essay; however, other thoughts and theories are fully described and skillfully analyzed.

Many problems of style in its stricter sense, that is the problems of expressing with appropriate and well-chosen words the feelings and ideas that are within us, are discussed by Beccaria with competence and subtlety. These qualities are shown, for instance, in his chapter on the use of adjectives, from which the following passages are excerpted:

> For objects having uniform and clear qualities it is better to choose adjectives which do not refer to the dominant qualities but to those which are less evident. For instance, it would be inadvisable to speak of *white snow,* since snow already brings up the idea of whiteness; it will be less objectionable to say *cold snow* because the adjective *cold* is not suggested immediately by the word *snow,* and because it does not exclude the perception of the first quality of whiteness which is implied in the word *snow;* and also because the adjective *cold* makes us suddenly feel something through another sense than sight, so that by saying *cold snow* we awaken two senses, while we awaken only one when we say *white snow.* But if we do not like *white snow* why are we pleased by the expression *white flake of snow?* It is because in the simple word *snow* we see a large white surface, and the stressing of this quality only adds to the uniformity of our feeling. But *flake* indicates a very small particle and therefore arouses a feeling of smallness; by adding to it the attribute of whiteness we fix in our imagination a quality that might have escaped us, since *flake* makes us think not so much of whiteness as of its shape and lightness.

> One thing a writer should avoid: the habit of having every noun accompanied by a faithful adjective, so that in a paragraph you may count as many adjectives as nouns. This type of writing ends by boring the reader because we do not pay attention to expected things; and the words which do not attract our attention are empty sounds without any meaning. . . . The best styles are those which vary continually the ways of presenting the largest possible number of feelings and thus maintain for a longer period an air of novelty and keep our attention always engaged; therefore, those adjectives should be used which are sudden and unexpected, and do not come according to regular patterns in obvious places.

Since style, esthetics, and psychology are necessarily interrelated, this book, more than being an essay on style, is an essay on human behavior, of which Beccaria was a keen observer. Besides the chapters on style itself, Beccaria is at his best in the chapter on human passions, in the analysis of the causes of laughter, in his theories on the evolution of language. But these are all like separate little essays, and there are sections of the book which are involved and abstruse. All in all, the unity that Beccaria saw in human knowledge seems to be missing in this work—a work with many ideas, but badly organized and lacking the systematic order and discipline of the treatise *On Crimes and Punishments*. Is this difference explained by the fact that for the first time in his writing career Beccaria was not stimulated by the congenial atmosphere of the Accademia dei Pugni? Or was the subject of the new essay less easy to coordinate and to view in its entirety? Possibly these and other reasons. In any case, let us not forget that almost all authors produce books of uneven quality, and Beccaria would soon again give us examples of more skillful writing.

As a book, *Research on the Nature of Style* was not a great success and the public showed only limited interest in it. Morellet, who had translated into French the treatise *On Crimes,* decided to translate the new book also, despite the fact that he found the contents "obscure." The French edition, under the title *Recherches sur le style,* appeared in Paris in 1771, about a year after the publication of the book in Italy; and the reception in France also was far from enthusiastic. Apart from this French version of Morellet, no other translation was made, but there have been reprints of the Italian text in several editions of Beccaria's writings.

During the period between his trip to Paris and his appointment to the chair of public economy in Milan Beccaria had also played with the idea of another project: a book on the development of civilization from the state of savagery to that of an organized society, with special emphasis on the gradual acceptance of a legal system as an important element of human progress. Beccaria had even thought of giving to this work the curious title of *Ripulimento delle nazioni,* meaning approximately: evolution toward the refinement of nations. But this work was never executed, at first because Beccaria decided to give precedence to his essay on style, and later because he became too busy with his teaching position. However, his serious intentions regarding this project are indicated by the many pages of notes that were found among Beccaria's papers. Following are some of the thoughts that he collected in preparation for the planned book:

> The antiquity of things has always produced in unthinking people an unreasoned veneration. This is so because unthinking people have the impression that only present things hurt them and they are not able to examine carefully whether their veneration for the old things is justified or not. It follows that when unthinking people are struck

by some misfortune they blame the present for it; while, on the contrary, many of the present evils may well be caused by things of the past that these people foolishly venerate.

Customs rarely arose from spontaneous decisions and agreements; more often they developed slowly because of some necessities. With the passing of time the necessities changed, but the customs remained unchanged because people had become used to them and because those who profited from them invented complicated tales about their origin, hiding from the people the true facts.

The wisdom of nations is almost always the fruit of their past unhappiness.

Not all that is useful to the public should necessarily be imposed, but all that is harmful to the public should be prohibited.

When physical causes are obscure, people are apt to think that the events they witness are the result of moral causes.

The attraction of men toward one pleasure instead of another is one of the main reasons for the difference in men's characters. These different tendencies are probably a consequence of the first pleasant feelings received by infants; grown-ups will look for the pleasures they first experienced as infants.

Religious opinions are good or bad not so much for the virtues they recommend or the vices they condemn, since in this they are all similar, but for the means they propose to use in order to reach their goals.

These are a few examples of thoughts found among Beccaria's papers; they probably date from the years 1766 to 1768, up to his appointment to the chair of economics at the Palatine School. He then became too busy with his new assignment and gave up the project for the book on the refinement of nations. This brings us back to that day of January 9, 1769, when the new department of economics at the Palatine School was officially inaugurated.

7

The Palatine School
and Elements of
Public Economy

FOR Milan the inauguration of the department of economics at the Palatine School was an important event. Beccaria delivered the address in the great hall of the school in front of Count Firmian and the élite of Milanese society. The new professor had asked and obtained permission to wear a regular suit instead of the academic gown which was customary on such special occasions. Beccaria spoke simply and clearly, without pomposity, and the audience was impressed by his thoughtfulness and serious approach. His prolusione greatly pleased Count Firmian and the vast majority of those present, as well as the many who read it as soon as it was printed. Copies were sent at once to Vienna by Count Firmian himself, while French and English translations made its contents known in wider circles.

The English translation of the prolusione was written by Sylvester Douglas, a young admirer of Beccaria who in 1767 had visited Milan and had had the opportunity of making Beccaria's personal acquaintance. Douglas, who was soon to enter public life and would later have a successful political career, wrote to Beccaria that he had decided to translate the prolusione in order to induce some young men from England to go to Milan and enroll in Beccaria's classes. The publisher,

Dodsley of London, printed Douglas's translation under the title *A Discourse on public oeconomy and commerce, by the Marquis Caesar Beccaria Bonesana.*[1]

The general reaction to Beccaria's speech was favorable. But there were a few discordant voices, and one of them was that of Pietro Verri, whose jealousy of his former friend was now increased by his conviction that somehow it was unfair of Beccaria to enter the field of economics, since this had long been Pietro's province. Also Pietro probably would have liked his brother Alessandro to obtain the new chair at the Palatine School. While praise came to Beccaria from many quarters, Pietro wrote to Alessandro on January 21, 1769, that Beccaria's inaugural speech was a collection of platitudes: "Now that he is on his own Beccaria reveals himself as very mediocre; in his long talk I couldn't find one single bright or new idea. . . . There were many labored and declamatory sentences, but no real eloquence."[2]

By then it would have been naive to expect a different judgment from the ever-bitter Pietro. In any case, Beccaria had not intended to use his inaugural speech as a platform from which to launch new ideas; for him the speech was above all an opportunity to indicate in a general way the scope of the new department and to stress the importance of economics in a world in which commerce, industry, and finance were developing at a fast pace.

Beccaria chose as the principal theme of his discourse a review of the long history of human civilization with special reference to economic evolution; and despite Pietro Verri's assertion, he not only spoke with warm eloquence, but he also expressed thoughts that were quite original. After defining public economy as the science that studies the means to preserve and increase the wealth of a state and to make the best use of it, Beccaria warned against studying one science while ignoring other fields of learning. Developing a point of view that he had already expressed in his *Research on the Nature of Style,* Beccaria said in his prolusione:

> Never will a man be great and illustrious in his science if he confines himself to that science and neglects others that have with it

---

1. See Beccaria, *Dei delitti e delle pene,* ed. Venturi, pp. 547–50.

2. For more details on Beccaria's inaugural speech at the Palatine School see Vianello, pp. 96–98, and Beccaria, *Opere,* ed. Romagnoli, vol. 1, pp. 363–64. For Pietro Verri's comments on the speech see *Carteggio di Pietro e di Alessandro Verri,* vol. 2, letter of January 21, 1769.

connections and analogies. An immense network binds all truths together: and they are more changeable, more uncertain and confused when their area is narrow and limited; they are instead simpler, larger, and more certain when they widen into a larger space and climb to a more eminent height.

In a way this statement parallels also the one made by Beccaria at the end of his plan for the teaching course, when he pointed out the usefulness of enlarging one's views by looking beyond the borders of one's own country. In all these statements there is a desire to encourage people to acquire an open mind and to broaden the basis of their knowledge. And although Beccaria was attracted by many sciences and was always in favor of scientific research in all fields, his humanistic spirit made him suspicious of specialization, which, if carried to extremes, could become counter-productive.

In his review of human evolution Beccaria made some bold statements which remind us of his treatise *On Crimes and Punishments* and of his stand for tolerance and civilized conduct among men. The history of mankind is filled with instances of evil deeds committed in the name of religion, and of selfish acts performed in the name of spiritual motives. Now Beccaria had the opportunity of castigating this kind of hypocrisy, to which man so often reverts. Speaking of the development of commerce toward the end of the Middle Ages, Beccaria mentioned the invention of the bill of exchange, a device that made unnecessary the transmission of cash from place to place in payment of trade debts. The bill of exchange was first used by Florentine Jews who wanted to avoid the dangers they faced when carrying with them large sums of money. In the Middle Ages it was unsafe for anyone to travel with much gold and silver in one's purse and it was doubly unsafe for Jewish merchants to do so in their journeys through Christian territories. Beccaria did not hesitate to express candidly what he had in mind:

> The Jews, persecuted not so much out of a misplaced religious zeal as out of greed inspired by their riches, resorted to the invention of the bill of exchange in order to make their wealth safe from arbitrary seizures; an important new era was thus opened for trading people, who saw their commercial exchanges become more rapid, safer, and more extensive.

Beccaria made another reference to religious zeal as an excuse for evil deeds when he came to speak of the Spanish conquests on the American continent. After pointing out the great attraction the gold of the New World had for the Spaniards, Beccaria added:

> Rivers of blood flowed, and millions of people were slain, sacrificed in theory to the religion of a God of peace, but in reality to the avidity for a metal that is the symbol of all pleasures. This easy and cruel conquest of gold made its possessors inept and neglectful of their arts and resources, so that soon the precious metal passed from the idle hands of the Spaniards into those of the more industrious people of Holland, England, and France.

Some of the most bigoted people in the audience did not like these passages in Beccaria's prolusione. But the majority did applaud the speech, and Beccaria's career as a professor of economics had a successful and promising start.[3]

The Course in Public Economy

A few weeks after the opening address, the regular course began, and Beccaria's classes were among the most popular in the Palatine School. Over a hundred students enrolled in his course, and only a few left during the two-year term. Beccaria's teaching followed fairly closely the preliminary plan that he himself had set for it; he made some changes, however, and added to the plan a concluding part on public order and security, so that the course was rearranged in the following five sections: (1) general principles of economics, (2) agriculture and industry, (3) commerce and banking, (4) taxation, (5) public order and security.

Beccaria dictated his lessons to the students from his own notes and, despite being urged by Prince Kaunitz and Count Firmian to collect them in book form, he never did. It is true that later on, in 1771, Beccaria wrote to Prince Kaunitz that his notes needed only a little polishing to be printed, but even then nothing was done. The principal reason for Beccaria's reluctance was that he had intended these lessons to be just that: lessons of economics and not a treatise on economics. Since they were lessons, he was often able to digress into related subjects, make philosophical and human considerations of a more general

---

3. For the reaction of the audience to the controversial passages in Beccaria's prolusione see Beccaria, *Opere,* ed. Romagnoli, vol. 1, pp. xcii–xciii; also Pietro Verri's letter of January 21, 1769.

character, or linger on some matters that appealed to him. This approach made his course highly personal, lively, and imaginative.

Beccaria's notes—or rather a transcribed version of them, since the original manuscript was not located until much later—were published a few years after his death under the title *Elementi di economia pubblica* (*Elements of Public Economy*). The last two chapters which were announced in Beccaria's plan, those on taxation and public order, were not found among the notes, and some critics thought that they had been lost. But one of the best scholars of Beccaria, Eugenio Landry, was undoubtedly right in saying that those two parts simply had been dropped by Beccaria as not essential to his course. This view has been corroborated in more recent times by Professor Mario Romani, who has ascertained that the original manuscript (kept in the Ambrosiana Library of Milan) supports Landry's judgment. It is clear, then, that in his course Beccaria preferred to dwell longer on problems that in his view were more important than those of taxation and public order. This explains Beccaria's remark at the end of his notes: "There would be other things to consider at this point, but lack of time compels me to conclude our discussions here."

The first Italian edition of *Elements of Public Economy* was published in Milan by Pietro Custodi in 1804. A second Italian edition was published in 1822 and other editions were published later—all based on the transcribed notes. Since the original manuscript contains several revisions in Beccaria's hand which do not appear in the transcribed version, it is to be hoped that future editions of the book will take all these corrections into account. The delay in the printing of the first Italian edition may explain the fact that the book was never translated into any other language.

We find in *Elements of Public Economy* a clear and detailed picture of Beccaria's thoughts as they were presented during his two-year course at the Palatine School. Because of its informality the book is very readable and entertaining, and it is easy to understand why Beccaria's course was so popular with the students and why his lessons were followed with great interest by a wide public outside the school. The economist Giuseppe Pecchio, writing soon after the publication of Beccaria's book, said that if he wanted to mark the passages in it that fascinated him the most he would have to mark every sentence. And Sergio Romagnoli added more recently: "This is one of the few books on economics that anyone can read, enjoying its contents from beginning to end."[4]

No one expected that in his course Beccaria would put forward economic doctrines of his own. Indeed, he could not have done this in a regular school, where a polemical or controversial stand would have been out of place. Besides, Beccaria was not an innovator in the economic field and in his course he wanted primarily to present theories and principles already advanced by others. In doing so, however, he expressed personal ideas which often opened new vistas on some aspects of the problems under discussion. Public economy, unlike mathematics, cannot be an exact science. It is a science that can be approached in different ways and admits different solutions in accordance with the temperament, the desires, and the feelings of those who are called on to study its problems. Beccaria, therefore, had a certain freedom of choice, and he exercised it by siding with the physiocratic school, which at that time represented the most liberal wing in the economic field. The first teacher of economics in Italy, Antonio Genovesi, had instead seen merits in the mercantile theory which tended toward protectionism and a state-regulated economy. It must be said, however, that Genovesi had been teaching in Naples, and his tendency toward protectionism is explained partly by his desire to offer the best solution for the weak economy of the Neapolitan kingdom.[5]

In the eighteenth century there was much hope that, once the right formula was found, the economic problems would be easily solved. Beccaria himself, having adhered to the physiocratic theories, seemed convinced that everything would work well under those principles. It may be noted that this point of view was shared by another Italian economist, no less than Pietro Verri, then working on his own book on economics. The physiocrats sponsored the doctrine of noninterference: the least possible intervention on the part of the government

---

4. See Pecchio, *Storia dell'economia pubblica in Italia,* p. 125, and Beccaria *Opere,* ed. Romagnoli, vol. 1, p. xciii. For more information about the various Italian editions of *Elements of Public Economy* see Beccaria, *Opere,* ed Romagnoli, vol. 2, p. 921.

5. Antonio Genovesi (1712–69) wrote *Lezioni di commercio,* considered the first complete and systematic work on economics in Italian. Despite their different views Genovesi was greatly admired by Beccaria. Pietro Verri, who had had early praises for Genovesi, later became critical of him for what Verri considered an excessive attachment to religious ideas and a lack of clear principles (see Venturi, p. 635).

in the economic sphere, the least possible impediment to the free flow of merchandise within certain areas. The physiocratic school had been founded by the Frenchmen François Quesnay and Jean de Gournay. The members of the group called themselves *les économistes,* until P.S. Dupont de Nemours proposed to call them by the more specific appellation of *physiocrates.* Their motto "laissez faire, laissez passer" appealed to many enlightened statesmen and scholars of the economically advanced countries, who saw in the physiocratic theories a promise of increased trade and economic progress. To be sure, there were limitations in the liberalism of the physiocrats: agriculture was for them the fundamental activity of man, and their theory of free trade applied principally to the basic agricultural products. In the agricultural field itself the physiocratic doctrine did not have a universal character, but allowed for restrictions and barriers at the borders of one's country.

Beccaria diverged somewhat from the physiocratic doctrine in the importance he gave to industry and commerce. For Beccaria these two activities were, like agriculture, essential elements of a national economy. But even Beccaria did not go very far with the idea of free trade. The fact that the Austrian empire was a very large unit may explain his inability to envision free trade on an international basis. He did not hesitate, for instance, to affirm that a nation should impose high duties on the importation of industrial products and low duties on the entrance of raw materials in order to encourage the development of domestic industry and make it difficult for foreign products to compete with it. He thus made the common mistake of forgetting that other countries can do the same or can retaliate in other ways.

It has been said that Beccaria's lectures anticipated in a remarkable way the conclusions of Adam Smith. This is true in the sense that Beccaria set out some principles that were later incorporated in Smith's economic doctrine: for instance, the usefulness of the division of labor and the necessity of the maximum return from labor as a condition of low costs. In pointing out the importance of labor as an element of production, Beccaria also indicated the possibility of determining the value of a product by figuring out the part, measured in work hours, that labor has in fashioning it. All these ideas, in various forms, may be found in the great work of Adam Smith, *Inquiry into the Nature and Causes of the Wealth of Nations,* which was to be published several years later, in 1776. But Smith, who had lived for some time in Paris before returning to Scotland, had many sources for his much more elaborate theories, one of these being indeed the physiocratic doctrine, of which he accepted certain parts while discarding others. It is doubtful that Adam Smith was influenced directly by Beccaria, but the precedence of the Milanese writer in some of Smith's ideas is certainly noteworthy.

It has also been said that Beccaria anticipated Malthus in his concern with the relationship between the growth of population and the means of subsistence. This is undoubtedly true, as we can see from the following passages from Beccaria's *Elements of Public Economy:*

> Excessive population becomes a liability to a nation when there is not enough work for all the people; this is due to the fact that the idle inhabitants must be fed at the expense of the useful population.

> It is necessary to point out that the population in a territory has certain natural limits which cannot be passed. Man is able to live and propagate as long as there are products that can feed him. These products come from the earth, and the earth can increase its production up to a point and not beyond it. Besides, man needs the help of other animals, and part of the earth's products is consumed by them. Therefore, the population can increase as long as the means of subsistence increase. These means may be augmented in a certain area thanks to a more perfected system of agriculture, or to the importation of products from other areas in exchange for services or work done in behalf of the foreign exporters—whose number, however, cannot increase beyond their own means of subsistence.

> They delude themselves who have as their only aim the multiplication of people and think that the population can increase indefinitely and that a large population is enough to assure the prosperity of a nation. It is clear, instead, that the population can grow only if the means of subsistence grow, and that the means do not grow as a consequence of the population increase.

These observations by Beccaria are all the more remarkable for having been made in a period in which the size of the world population was almost stable and no one could foresee the magnitude and complexity of this problem in later times. There is no doubt that Beccaria's ideas opened the way to further useful considerations on the relationship between population and means of subsistence, but we do not know what direct influence, if any, these ideas had on Malthus's *Essay on Population*. Certainly Malthus went further in the exploration of the possible consequences of an unchecked population increase, and he arrived at a pessimistic outlook on future developments that we do not find in Beccaria.

These observations on population are only one example of the comments made by Beccaria on many problems more or less closely connected with his subject—comments which make his *Elements of Public Economy* a lively and interesting book to read.[6] Of course, Beccaria saw the economic problems as they appeared in the eighteenth century, but from a human and literary point of view this rather enhances the interest of the reader who, through the book, has a picture of the life, attitudes, and customs of that period. Beccaria may not always be above criticism in his economic theories, as for instance in his view on international exchanges of which we have already spoken; but his ideas are always stimulating and his descriptions of facts and situations are often entertaining and picturesque. His discussions opened the way to the study of subjects which at that time were largely unexplored, such as psychology and sociology; and the variety of his interests made it possible for him to see related points in different fields and to make interesting considerations on the basic aspects of human life.

Concerning other points he touched upon in his *Elements of Public Economy,* the problems of population seem to have fascinated Beccaria from many different points of view besides the one already mentioned. He speaks with poetical warmth of the institution of marriage and thinks that the family is not only a useful element of society, but is above all a desirable union that gives joy and security to its members. Beccaria has little sympathy for men who choose to remain bachelors, as he thinks that a large number of single men in a society is bound to increase licentiousness and moral corruption. Neither has he great sympathy for religious celibacy, which in his opinion should be limited to those who are clearly inspired by a spiritual vocation and voluntarily prefer that status to any other. He condemns without reservation the habit of confining men and women to a life of seclusion because of financial considerations, such as the interest of certain families to keep their properties intact for reasons of power and prestige. This was an accepted custom at that time, and Beccaria had seen

---

6. For the complete Italian text of *Elements of Public Economy* see Beccaria, *Opere,* ed. Romagnoli, vol. 1, pp. 379–649 (chapter on population, pp. 401–33).

it adopted in his own family, as his father's brothers and sisters had had to enter religious orders. Beccaria considers this habit not only cruel, but potentially harmful if too many young people are thus taken away from productive life. In this case, says Beccaria, the sovereign of a nation should have the right, in the interest of his country, to put some restrictions on this practice.

Another aspect of population that fascinates Beccaria and appeals to his mathematical mind is statistics on human life. He presents tables of mortality and life expectancy based on data collected in various countries. Those figures are of interest even today because they show the progress made in life expectancy at birth since Beccaria's time, progress due in large part to the reduction of infant mortality. Life expectancy after infancy, on the other hand, does not seem to have changed considerably since the eighteenth century.

Not only does Beccaria like to present curious facets of the population statistics, but he tries to find out and explain the reasons for certain situations and trends: why, for instance, men and women live longer in the countryside than in the large cities, why there is more infant mortality in France than in England and Holland, why monks and nuns have a low rate of mortality when young and a high rate when they reach forty-five or fifty, why on the average women live longer than men, and so on.

Beccaria's social aims are often evident. For example, in the long chapter on agriculture Beccaria speaks with compassionate eloquence of the poverty and ignorance in which the large majority of peasants live. He proposes several steps to help improve their condition, first among them a better education. Peasants do not need long and difficult studies, says Beccaria, but they all should learn to read, write, and do some arithmetic; they should also learn some basic facts about their own profession, so as to be able to have a certain order in their ideas and to understand and accept new agricultural methods and technical improvements. It would be good, adds Beccaria, if the parish priests who live among the peasants could teach them some useful facts about practical matters instead of confining themselves to a theology "which is always respectable but is often useless when presented to the simple souls of uneducated peasants."

Beccaria also proposes the establishment of academies of agricultural research for studying ways of improving the production and fertility of the soil, for printing and distributing to the peasants instructions on many useful subjects, and for organizing competitions and prizes for the best crops. It may be noted that these proposals, quite unusual for that time, were adopted later, in one form or another, by every civilized country.

At the end of his chapter on agriculture Beccaria stresses the necessity of seeing the problems of agriculture within the general economy of a nation because all economic activities are interdependent. Here Beccaria forgets smaller considerations of national rivalries and, as if having a sudden vision of a better future world, says:

> We come now to a useful thought, that a nation can prosper at the expense of another only to a certain point; beyond that point our prosperity, in order to be a real one, must bring about the prosperity of others, because it is impossible to be happy or to be miserable in isolation: a sign, this, of a community of things, of a tacit brotherhood that nature has decreed for the whole human species. This thought of a universal brotherhood should lead us to a virtuous path —away from the narrow and petty views of selfish gain, toward the serene areas of justice and goodwill.

Another interesting thought is expressed by Beccaria when he discusses the subject of forestry and insists on the necessity of preventing the indiscriminate cutting of trees for commercial purposes. The destruction of forests, says Beccaria, is less easily repaired than is the destruction of other cultivations, because it takes a long time for trees to grow again and also because the damage in this case may have harmful consequences to many industries and activities which rely for their existence on an abundant and conveniently located supply of wood. Although Beccaria is a supporter of the laissez faire formula in the economic field, he thinks that there should be limits to this doctrine when a whole society is bound to suffer from its application. To the objection that if the principle of private property is accepted the owners of forests are entitled to do what they want with them, Beccaria answers that there is no such absolute right of property in the first place. We may recall that in his treatise *On Crimes and Punishments* Beccaria had described the right of property as "a terrible and perhaps unnecessary right." To be exact, in the manuscript of the treatise and in its first edition the right of property was described as "a terrible, but perhaps necessary right." In later editions this expression was changed to "a terrible and perhaps unnecessary right" and this form was the final one. Cantù thinks that the two versions show a change in Beccaria's attitude, but in effect the distinction is more a question of form than of substance.[7] The fact is that Beccaria had doubts about the necessity, or legitimacy, of the right of property. In this his view was certainly far from that of Blackstone, who unhesitatingly described the right of property as "one of the absolute rights, inherent in every Englishman."

At any rate, whether for Beccaria the right of property is necessary or not, he does not deny its validity; he states only that there must be limitations in the ways it may be used, and in Beccaria's opinion the harm done by the destruction of forests shows why certain regulations restricting the right of property are justified even in a system of economic freedom. Beccaria explains why he thinks these limitations are historically justified:

> There can be no doubt that property is the daughter and not the mother of society. Before the union of men and families there was uncertain and precarious possession, not certain and assured property; there was use of things but without a definite right. The idea of this right came later as the result of a tacit agreement, due to common interests and circumstances, that gave the possessions of each man the assurance of a common defense against encroachments by any single member of the community. This being the origin of the right of property, it is clear that property is subjected to the laws, written or unwritten, which have as their purpose the common good and general usefulness.

Beccaria adds that these laws must have a universal character and that the same potential limitations must apply to all properties. In accordance with this view Beccaria states that if the free and indiscriminate cutting of trees is shown to be harmful to society, then the right, the necessity, and the convenience of forest conservation will be demonstrated. And how will this conservation be regulated? As a rule, says Beccaria, as much timber should be allowed to be cut in a year as the quantity that grows in the same period, although complete surveys and precise regulations would be advisable in order to establish a rational utilization of the resources in all possible circumstances. In Beccaria's opinion, as we may see, complete economic freedom is not always to be recommended; and he does not hesitate to uphold the necessity of similar restrictive clauses in the regulations dealing with hunting and fishing.

---

7. See Cantù, p. 127n.

Another point that Beccaria stresses repeatedly is the importance of scientific studies, which in his time were rather neglected: this was especially true of practical sciences such as chemistry, botany, and mineralogy. The research in these areas, says Beccaria, may help us to find more rational methods of production in the industrial and agricultural fields; and the study of fossils, metals, and minerals may enable us to penetrate many secrets of nature and lead us toward great inventions and discoveries. Although many members of the old generation in Beccaria's time considered these studies childish and useless, quite a few of the young men were eager to enter these fields. Beccaria is all in favor of them, and he asks the conservative elements of society to have an open mind and not to discourage the young people from their endeavors.

In his course Beccaria frequently shows his sense of humor, already apparent in his early articles for *Il Caffè*. For instance, after stating that the search for pleasure is an element of human conduct, Beccaria notes that some may point out examples of people who did not look for pleasure in life: for instance, the ancient Spartans who were known for their austerity and for their hostility to all pleasures. But the Spartans did not really contradict the general rule: for them, explains Beccaria, the greatest pleasure consisted in being enclosed in heavy and threatening armor, surrounded by crashing swords and lances, in the midst of the groaning wails of vanquished enemies. Therefore, we may still say that the search for pleasure is common to all men.

It is regrettable that Beccaria's lectures were not published soon after the course was held, but in any case we know that his classes were followed attentively not only by his numerous students, but by government officials and other interested people. One of these was Pietro Verri, who read regularly the notes of one of Beccaria's students. As has already been mentioned, Pietro Verri was then writing his own book on economics, which was published in 1771 under the title *Meditazioni sull'economia politica*. Beccaria had then already completed his first and only two-year course. Pietro, who did not hesitate to follow Beccaria's classes, was very careful not to let his former friend know what he himself was writing. Yet once his book was about to be published, Pietro wrote to his brother Alessandro, on January 23, 1771: "Beccaria is not so haughty anymore; a few days ago I saw him and talked to him. He was so nice, just as he used to be. We talked about economics, and without boasting I can say that of the two it was not he who seemed to be a teacher. I talked freely because by now he is not in time to steal my ideas."

Beccaria was not in time and, of course, had no intention of stealing Pietro's ideas. Pietro's book, we may point out, was quite a success: in two years it was reprinted six times, and it was translated into French, German, and Dutch.

Pietro and Beccaria were not too far apart in their views on economics, since both adhered to the principles of free enterprise and had drawn their main ideas from the physiocratic doctrine. Both accepted, as a practical measure, the necessity of duties and restrictions in commercial exchanges; but both had at the same time a larger vision of an open world in which international trade would flourish for the benefit of all. "If all nations could abolish their customs duties," wrote Verri, "this would certainly be of great reciprocal advantage. Nations would be nearer to each other, commerce would increase, industry would be spurred to greater production, and people would enjoy greater comforts. But as long as other countries put restrictions on our goods we must do the same toward theirs." This aspiration on the part of Verri corresponds to Beccaria's belief that all nations are interdependent and that one cannot be prosperous indefinitely if the prosperity is not shared by other nations.

But although Pietro Verri and Beccaria were near each other in their ideas, they were quite different in temperament and in method. Verri was more concrete and more specific than Beccaria. He never left anything in midair: he examined all questions thoroughly and proposed clear and practical solutions. Beccaria was less persevering; sometimes he touched on a problem and hinted at a solution without going further. But there was always a human touch in Beccaria, which gave a philosophical quality to his economic thought. He never lost sight of wider horizons and of the principle he enunciated in his inaugural address: namely that no science is isolated, for all truths are tied together in an immense network. With the passing of time some of his specific views lost their validity, but because of his general approach Beccaria's *Elements of Public Economy* has maintained a special place among writings on economic subjects, while studies by other authors seem to have aroused only a temporary interest.[8]

8. For some comments on the similarities and differences in the views of Beccaria and Pietro Verri in the field of economics see Vianello, pp. 150–66, and Beccaria, *Opere,* ed. Romagnoli, vol. 1, p. 382. For more details consult Pecchio, *Storia dell'economia pubblica in Italia.*

8

The Economic
Council of Milan

BECCARIA did not hold for long his position as professor of economics in the Palatine School. After completing the first two-year course he became restless about his work and eager for a change. His teaching position, important as it was, was badly remunerated, and he was now in a rather precarious financial situation, as shown by his letters to the book dealer Chirol of Geneva, which indicate that he was unable to pay for the books he had ordered. Besides, once the first two-year course had been completed, the next courses would be repetitive and much less rewarding for a creative mind. Great as his desire had been to teach at the Palatine School, Beccaria now began to look at the Supreme Economic Council of Milan as the organization that he would like to join in an important capacity. The council had been established in 1765 as a consultative body which would propose laws and regulations in the economic field and cooperate with the central government in the solution of local problems. Beccaria thought that he had a good opportunity to enter the council because its president was his old friend, Count Gian Rinaldo Carli, who was very well disposed toward him. It is true that Pietro Verri was then one of the council members, but it was unlikely that he would oppose openly Beccaria's candidacy against Carli's favorable stand. In any case, the final decision would be made in Vienna. After the end of his first course at the Palatine School, Beccaria decided to write to the chancellor, Prince Kaunitz, in the Austrian capital:

> Although only two years have elapsed since I began to fulfill to the best of my ability the duties entrusted to me as an instructor of public economy, I think I may rely on your generous feelings and express to you my great and constant desire to put myself and my knowledge of political and economic matters more directly and completely at Her Majesty's service. For this reason I take the liberty of asking Your Highness to take into consideration my wish to enter the Supreme Economic Council of this city when a vacancy should occur, since the purpose and functions of the said council are in direct line with my principal studies. As regards the selection of another person to succeed me in the chair of public economy in this school, I beg to inform Your Highness that in these two years I have trained more than one pupil who, with the help of my notes—which need only a little polishing to be printed—and of my direct assistance, would be able to take over the teaching until Her Majesty may decide otherwise. This I dare to submit to Your Highness with the confidence of an honest man who relies completely on the decisions of a great and beneficent minister.

Prince Kaunitz, so gracefully praised, was indeed favorably inclined and by the decree of April 29, 1771, Beccaria, who was now thirty-three, was appointed a full member of the Supreme Economic Council of Milan, or simply the Economic Council, as it was soon to be called.[1]

The new appointment meant a much higher salary for Beccaria. At the beginning, however, in addition to his new duties he was asked to continue his teaching at the Palatine School. Beccaria had favored as his successor one of his former pupils, Giuseppe Biumi, but there were other candidates as well, and finally the appointment went to Alfonso Longo, who was then teaching public law at the same Palatine School. At the time of *Il Caffè* Longo had been one of its contributors and later, at the time of the break between the Verris and Beccaria, he had tried to remain friendly with both parties. In his letter to Prince Kaunitz, Beccaria had spoken of a possible printing

---

1. The new Italian name for the economic council of Milan was *Magistrato Camerale*. This was mostly a change of name, since the functions and personnel of the council remained the same.

of his notes on political economy because he thought that this would make it easier for his former pupil Biumi to take over the teaching. Now that Longo had been appointed to the job the printing of the notes in book form seemed no longer necessary and, as we know, it took many years before they were finally published. Although his relationship with Longo was fairly friendly, Beccaria was probably a little unhappy about the appointment, not only because he would have liked to help Biumi, but also because Longo was not yet able to replace Beccaria in view of his other duties in the school. In fact, in order to assure the continuity of the course of economics Beccaria had to do one more full year of teaching; and only in 1772 was he finally able to devote all his time to the new career as a public official.

Beccaria's life was far from easy at this time, and Pietro Verri told his brother that their former friend had become "apathetic, lost in his thoughts, oppressed by small details." There were reasons for Beccaria's behavior. For one thing, his wife's health was far from satisfactory: her constant fever and gradual weakening were symptoms of a consumptive disease. She now stayed almost always in the country where the air was purer, while Beccaria remained in Milan. "Please get better soon," wrote Cesare in 1773, "I wish that that cursed fever would disappear; the sooner I see you, the better I will feel."

Beccaria was also preoccupied with his financial situation, which was still bad despite the better salary that he was beginning to earn. His sister, Maddalena, had found a husband, but the family had little cash available and had gone into debt in order to provide a dowry. Moreover, Beccaria's two younger brothers, Francesco and Annibale, were already planning legal action against Cesare in the event that their father did not treat them fairly in the disposal of the estate.

Teresa's health grew progressively worse, and then the sad event occurred: she died, at the age of twenty-nine, on March 14, 1774, one day before Cesare's thirty-sixth birthday. Soon after her death, Pietro Verri wrote to his brother: "Beccaria now lives in Calderara's home. He says that sorrow doesn't do any good; this is true, but in this case it shows that his sensibility is limited. I am sure that not six months will pass before we will see him married again: he cannot survive without a support."

Pietro Verri was right, and it took not six months but barely six weeks for Beccaria to be deeply involved in a new relationship, this time with a lady by the name of Anna Barbò, daughter of Count Barnaba Barbò. Some of her letters have been preserved, but not those of Beccaria to her.[2]

Here is Anna's letter of May 3, 1774, written only a month and a half after Teresa's death:

My beloved:

Your warm letter arouses in me a very strong love and I cannot tell you how happy I am when I hear your voice or I see in writing your sweet words. I want then to speed up the accomplishment of our happiness and to be soon in possession of your dear person, the sole object of my desire. The ardor that I feel for you fills me so completely that I am unable to describe it; you see that it is not my fault if I am so confused, for you are the cause of it. . . . I can only offer you again my heart, of which you are the only owner. My dear joy, I embrace you and tonight I will give you the fifty caresses I promised you.

Your lover and spouse, Anna Barbò

Two days later:

My handsome and beloved Cesarino, remember that I am your very faithful spouse. When you come this afternoon please bring with you the key to the theater box; it may be that this will make my mother decide to go to the theater, and this would please me immensely because I would then be able to enjoy in peace the company of my treasure.

The theater mentioned in this letter, and in the one that follows, was undoubtedly the Ducal Theater, the only one then open in Milan. La Scala was at that time in the planning stage and would not be ready until 1778.

On May 7 Anna wrote:

I see that you kissed my letter and that you would have preferred to do that to the one who wrote it. I am sure that this is true, since I have had enough proofs not to doubt it. . . . I enjoy the thought that

---

2. For Anna Barbò's letters, quoted in the original Italian, see Vianello, *La vita e l'opera di Cesare Beccaria,* pp. 102–7. These letters, as well as many other letters and documents concerning Beccaria, are kept in the Ambrosiana Library of Milan.

tonight we will go to the theater and that our hearts will be together in our little corner.

The marriage took place on June 4, 1774, two months and a half after Teresa's death. For those convinced that Beccaria was sincerely attached to Teresa until the end, it is not easy to explain his marriage to another woman so soon after his loss. Some of Beccaria's friends, like Lambertenghi, expressed the opinion that he simply hated solitude and needed a new companion. This undoubtedly is true, and it is also true that the new wife came from a respectable and wealthy family, in a position to put some order in Beccaria's financial situation. But these could not have been the main reasons for the new marriage. The fact is that Beccaria fell sincerely and deeply in love with Anna Barbò, as can be seen from her letters and other people's comments. During the courtship Pietro Verri wrote to his brother: "Beccaria is now a languishing suitor, shamefully in love."

We cannot exclude the possibility, despite the affection Beccaria showed toward Teresa all through her illness, that his feelings for her had weakened with the passing of time; but the fact remains that the relationship between Beccaria and Anna Barbò started very soon after Teresa's death. Certainly Teresa's brother, Michele, who in that period was on a trip abroad, must have felt quite a shock when he received at the same time the news of his sister's death and of his brother-in-law's new marriage. Having always felt very friendly toward Cesare, he wrote him a kind and understanding letter, from which we quote:

> I can't tell you how sad I felt at the news of my sister's death. As much as I try to overcome the blow, it isn't at all easy because there were very strong ties between her and me due to our sharing the same education, our being brought up together, our friendship. I remember her so vividly and so perfectly that I still hope to see her some day; then I realize that this hope is vain and unreasonable, and I fall again into a profound sadness. But since my sorrow is useless and my condolences would only arouse in your soul some thoughts that would disturb the serenity that I wish for you, I prefer not to talk of this and, instead, I want to congratulate you for having proceeded to a second marriage which I hope will be gladdened by a thousand happinesses and satisfactions. Please do not think that I disapprove of your prompt resolution; on the contrary, I would have condemned the opposite if, in order to conform to some old and ridiculous opinions, you had postponed the carrying out of your decision. I fully

realize that your occupations and your studies do not give you the possibility of applying to family affairs those cares that you so successfully devote to the well-being of your country and of mankind. This is what I think, and certainly I will never ascribe to your decision a motive less worthy of your character. . . . I will always feel honored to be your brother-in-law and to have your continuous friendship, as well as that of your new, respected wife.[3]

What can one say of this generous attitude? Perhaps that we all should accept this event in the same spirit, without trying to analyze or explain all the feelings and impulses of a human being. We may add here that Beccaria and Michele Blasco remained good friends for the rest of their lives.[4]

While Beccaria was faced with all kinds of problems and events in his private life, he was fulfilling competently and conscientiously his new duties as a member of the economic council. This was an important body whose proposals in the economic field, submitted by its members either individually or jointly as the case might be, were weighed carefully by the central authorities and paved the way to useful reforms in line with the general policy of the government. Although the final decisions always were made in the Austrian capital, the Milan council was asked to give its opinion on all the important projects, so that the new regulations, when enacted, would conform as much as possible to local needs. Other councils in other provinces of the empire had similar functions.

The files of the Milan council show us that Beccaria soon became one of its most active and authoritative members—together with Gian Rinaldo Carli, Pietro Verri, Paolo Frisi, and a few others—and that his suggestions and interventions had a considerable influence on the government's decisions. Besides being the member in charge of all regulations concerning the food supplies in Milan and its province,

---

3. Teresa's brother, Michele Blasco, was a professional soldier, as his father had been. His letter to Beccaria is dated June 28, 1774; for the original text see Cantù, pp. 122–23n.

4. Beccaria remained grateful to Michele Blasco for his kind attitude at the time of Beccaria's second marriage. In 1779 Michele went to Vienna to apply for a new position in the military administration, and Beccaria supported his application with a warm letter to Baron Sperges, still in charge of Italian affairs under Chancellor Kaunitz. Baron Sperges, always friendly toward Beccaria, did his best to help Michele in his career. See Beccaria, *Opere,* ed. Romagnoli, vol. 2, pp. 909, 936; also Landry, p. 249n.

Beccaria was asked by the central government to study many other economic and financial problems, and his reports were not only informative and accurate, but also resourceful and imaginative. The papers he presented were thoughtful essays, highly appreciated by the authorities and by his colleagues in the council who collaborated with him in the preparation of some of them. These reports have been published in the Italian editions of Beccaria's works, but they have never appeared in English.[5]

Already in 1771, while he was still a professor at the Palatine School, Beccaria was asked to prepare a plan for a new piece of legislation on the bills of exchange and, soon after, a plan for monetary reform. Such reform was badly needed because the lack of clear regulations in this field had caused inconveniences and obstacles to the economic development of the region. It may be recalled that the first essay written by Beccaria at the time of the Accademia dei Pugni, in 1762, had been a study of monetary problems in Milan, which, despite some technical errors, already pointed the way toward a more rational monetary system. Now, ten years after that first essay, Beccaria presented a new plan which became the basis for more detailed studies by a commission for monetary reform.

Beccaria himself participated in the work of this commission; the problems, however, were fairly complex and, as we will see, it took several years for new monetary laws to be enacted. In the meantime Beccaria wrote several other reports and one of them, on the consumption of grain in the province of Milan, was prepared in cooperation with Pietro Verri. The date of this paper was March 26, 1774, just the period between Teresa's death and Beccaria's second marriage. This study, requested by the government, showed that for several reasons a precise calculation of the consumption of grain in Milan was almost impossible, but it gave as accurate figures as possible on the basis of available data. This was the first piece of work

---

5. In the state archives of Milan and Vienna there are several still unpublished reports by Beccaria on various economic matters. Professor Mario Romani, director of the Institute of Economic and Social History at the Catholic University of Milan, has been studying these documents with the help of his staff and he plans to publish them as soon as the work is completed. Professor Romani has kindly provided us with a list of the reports examined so far. Although they concern for the most part problems of ordinary administration, their publication will nevertheless be useful, since it will complete, as far as possible, the collection of Beccaria's writings.

in which the two former friends collaborated after their long break. From then on Pietro Verri's attitude toward Beccaria softened somewhat and, although he continued to talk about him without affection, he now showed more disdain than jealousy or animosity. The two men saw each other every day, worked in the same office, and often had to discuss together the problems submitted to them. Having, after all, a common goal in their work, they exchanged their points of view and gradually began to feel a little closer to each other. Of course, it was Pietro Verri who had taken the initiative in breaking off their friendship and it was now he who began to see that Beccaria perhaps did not deserve all the insults that he had been secretly addressing to him all these years. Some hostility was still there, however, and when, a few months later, Beccaria's new wife became pregnant, Pietro recounted this news to his brother, adding: "Beccaria is only a shadow of the sublime man he used to be, you wouldn't recognize in him the philosopher who had in his hand the approving votes of all Europe." Evidently, Pietro had not yet digested the innocent boast in the letter that Beccaria had written to him from Paris many years before!

During this period Beccaria wrote some interesting studies on practical ways to assure the conservation of forests and to increase the production of mines in the Lombard region. As regards the forests, Beccaria proposed the adoption of several measures and regulations aimed at preventing the existing wood reserves from being depleted by excessive cutting. As to the mines, he pointed out the reasons for which the production in Lombardy was unsatisfactory, first among them the antiquated and costly systems of extraction and operation. To remedy the situation Beccaria suggested the transfer to Lombardy of some mine experts from Hungary and other parts of the empire where mining was much better organized. These experts, said Beccaria, would instruct the local operators on improved ways to do the work; moreover, he added, some of our young men who have studied mineralogy should be sent for a period to the more advanced provinces in order to see on the spot how the mines there are operated. This was quite a new idea for that time. The rest of the report contained a detailed presentation of technical elements, which shows the care and diligence with which Beccaria had studied these problems. These were matters, by the way, that Beccaria had discussed in his course at the Palatine

School, and now he had the opportunity of suggesting the steps necessary for putting his theoretical teachings into practice.

The monetary reform, based largely on Beccaria's recommendations, was finally enacted in 1777. We may recall that numerous coins of many countries had circulation in Milan. In very simple terms, the new regulations established the intrinsic value of each coin, based on its metallic content, and on this basis the rate of exchange among all the coins was determined. These fixed rates of exchange assured that all financial transactions would be free from undue risks and unfair deals by speculators. Beccaria, who had been a prominent member of the commission for the monetary reform, was now appointed supervisor of the mint, and at the beginning of 1778 he presented a report on the new monetary laws in which he reviewed all the advantages of the reform and made suggestions on how to cope with future problems, such as the introduction of new foreign coins whose metallic contents and value had not been officially established.

Beccaria's marriage with Anna turned out to be a successful one. A year after the wedding Pietro Verri wrote to Alessandro: "Beccaria has been lucky, he married a good young woman, wise and affectionate; she knows how to keep peace and goodwill in the home, and everybody likes her."

In 1778 Beccaria was forty years old and his son Giulio, born of his second marriage, was three. Of his daughters from the first marriage, Giulia was now eighteen, finishing her education in the monastery of San Paolo where her father had sent her rather incongruously, since he himself had complained years earlier that education in a religious institution had had on him a stifling effect. We will not try to give an explanation for all the inconsistencies in Beccaria's behavior: perhaps he thought that a religious education was good for a woman, perhaps he had other reasons. As for his second daughter, Maria, she was now fourteen and was kept home on account of her frailness and delicate health.

As we have seen, the relationship between Beccaria and Pietro Verri had gradually improved, but Pietro saw to it that it remained rather cool and formal. In Pietro's letters there is not a spark of real warmth when Beccaria is the subject. In 1778 Pietro wrote to Alessandro: "Beccaria has changed very much from what he used to be fourteen years ago. We are now on fairly friendly terms, and this reciprocal feeling is evident in all the council meetings that we attend. He is very timid, more than any of the women I am acquainted with."[6]

Shyness and reserve were, indeed, Beccaria's traits in his contacts with people. According to Pietro, Beccaria did not like to catch cold and was afraid of drafts, but he did not want people to notice it. "This fear that he tries to hide," says Pietro, "is typical of the contradictions in his character." In another letter, some time later, Pietro recalls the "air of superiority" that Beccaria had taken toward him after reaching literary fame. But Pietro wants to forget that attitude "because Beccaria is not really a bad man, only weak, and he is not malicious or deceitful; besides, he has a good sense of values and knows how to reason on many subjects." This is quite a change from Pietro's old outbursts; yet he adds in the same letter with cold detachment: "He has put on a lot of weight and seems always sleepy under so much fat; sometimes he is so absentminded that you have to repeat the same question two or three times."

We should always take Pietro's statements about Beccaria with some caution; but it was true, of course, that Beccaria had a tendency to obesity and that he had put on weight. Undoubtedly, he was also at times absentminded, and we know that he was rather negligent in his dress. Fortunately his sense of values was good and he knew how to reason, Pietro Verri himself had said so! To be sure the relationship between the two men had improved considerably, and this was partly due to Cesare's new wife, Anna, who became a good friend of Pietro Verri's wife and saw her frequently. The Scala Theater had just been inaugurated and the two ladies proposed to their husbands to rent a box together for the season. From then on, the two couples met regularly in the new theater—the pride of Milan for many years to come.

A New System of Weights and Measures

Around that time Beccaria was entrusted with a study that enabled him to write a report of historic importance. The Austrian government, having jurisdiction over vast territories, had tried for a long

---

6. This and other letters of the Verri brothers in this period are quoted from Vianello, *La vita e l'opera di Cesare Beccaria*, pp. 108 ff. The full text of these letters may be found in *Carteggio di Pietro e di Alessandro Verri*.

time to tackle one of its great problems: the confusion and complications that were caused by the multitude of systems of weights and measures that existed in the empire. Not only were the systems incredibly numerous—many of them existing in the same province—but the various standards were not always established with clarity and precision. This state of affairs was harmful to an efficient handling of commercial operations and other economic transactions. In order to remedy the situation the Viennese authorities decided to move gradually toward simpler and more rational systems of weights and measures, and as a first step it was decided to have no more than one system in any one of the Austrian dominions. There was no thought at that time of unifying the systems of the whole empire; this was a more ambitious goal to be left for a future time.

Of all the Austrian provinces Lombardy presented one of the most difficult and complicated situations, since at least twenty different measures and four weight systems were used in its small territory. As a first step it was decided to adopt the "Milanese arm" as the only measure of length in Lombardy, and Beccaria was entrusted with the task of doing all the preparatory work for the carrying out of this decision. He was asked also to study a larger project for the reduction to a uniform standard of all other measures and weights.[7]

Beccaria worked hard on this assignment, which appealed to him because it challenged his ingenuity and knowledge in various fields in which he had always been interested, especially mathematics and physics. He was determined to fulfill his task with the utmost diligence and, seeing how complex the work would be, he obtained the authorization to secure the cooperation and services of his colleague in the economic council, the mathematician Paolo Frisi, and of Beccaria's younger brother, Annibale, a skillful technician and mechanic. In passing, it is interesting to note that Cesare often tried to help his two brothers, recommending them for various jobs, without too much success and, as far as we know, without ever being thanked for his efforts.[8]

---

7. We have called "Milanese arm" the measure of length known in Italian as *braccio di fabbrica milanese;* it corresponds approximately to one yard.

8. Beccaria's other brother, Francesco, aspired to a military career. Cesare did his best to help him and recommended him to a high officer in Parma; the request was turned down, however, and Francesco promptly blamed Beccaria for the negative result. See Landry, pp. 156–58.

On January 25, 1780, Beccaria presented his report "On the reduction of the measures of length to uniformity in the state of Milan," and in it, first of all, he acknowledged the help of Professor Paolo Frisi for his accurate mathematical calculations and of his brother Annibale for his technical work. After explaining the great importance of this undertaking for the economic development of the region, Beccaria described the three steps he had taken in order to secure the adoption of the new standard, the Milanese arm, as the only legal unit of length in Lombardy. First, he had to build a model of the new standard that would be unalterable, lasting, solid, precise; this would be the model for all copies ever to be made. Second, he had to reduce all the old measures to the Milanese arm and make the tables showing the exact ratio between the new legal measure and all the old ones. Third, he had to submit a list of regulations to be obeyed by the public in order to insure the rapid and total adoption of the new standard.[9]

The problems to be solved in order to accomplish these three objectives are described in Beccaria's report. Briefly, he chose as the most suitable material for the model of the new measure a combination of wrought iron and silver, built and marked with the fractional subdivisions at a given temperature. This material had all the required qualities and was guaranteed against any alteration if held at the same original temperature. Besides the main standard to be kept in Milan, several copies were made for safekeeping in other towns of Lombardy in order to avoid the necessity of resorting to the main standard in case of disputes or controversies outside Milan. Periodical checks of the various copies against the main standard were suggested.

For the tables showing the ratio between the Milanese arm and all the old discarded measures it was necessary to collect standards of those measures, as precise as possible, and calculate the ratio not only for the various measures but for all their subdivisions. The calculations were made separately by Beccaria and his co-workers and, once the results had been verified, the final figures were listed in clear tables to be used by the public. These tables were to be printed in very large quantity and posted in all public places, stores, and mar-

---

9. For the complete text in Italian of Beccaria's report on the unification of the measures of length ("Della riduzione delle misure di lunghezza all'uniformità per lo Stato di Milano") see Beccaria, *Opere,* ed. Romagnoli, vol. 2, pp. 173–209.

kets; the expense for the printing was to be partly recovered by the sale of the tables to private people at a small charge.

Recalling that an attempt at some reforms in the field of weights and measures had been made in 1604 and that it had failed for lack of firmness on the part of the authorities, Beccaria suggested that this time there should be a clear prohibition against dealers' using the abolished measures; moreover, that contracts containing clauses mentioning the old measures should be considered null and void, that no price should ever relate in the future to old measures, and that penalties should be established for those violating the new regulations.

Up to this point Beccaria had described in his report the practical work done for the unification of the measures of length in Lombardy. Now he made some preliminary suggestions for similar solutions as to the measures of area and capacity, and as to the weight standards. He proposed to reduce to only one the standards used in Milan in each category and to extend these Milanese standards to the rest of Lombardy, so that there would be only one standard for each category in the whole province. He admitted that too much change might not be advisable at the moment, but suggested, nevertheless, some rectifications in the Milanese standards in order to relate the measures of capacity to the units of weight.

With these proposals Beccaria had completed the task entrusted to him by the government, and his report could have ended there. But he was not satisfied and, although he knew that too much change was not possible at that time, he decided to describe the ideal solution he had in mind for the future, not only for Lombardy, but for the whole world: a solution which embodies two great ideas, the decimal system and a universal standard of all measures and weights in mutual relationship.

Although these ideas had never been outlined clearly before Beccaria, they had been the object of past studies and experiments. For example, a system having a kind of relationship among measures of length, volume, and capacity had been adopted in the kingdom of Naples in the fifteenth century. Then, around 1600, the Dutch mathematician Simon Stevin had developed the use of decimal fractions and predicted that the universal introduction of decimal coinage, measures, and weights was only a question of time. In the seventeenth century the French astronomer Jean Picard had proposed to take as a unit of length that of a pendulum swinging once every second at sea level, at a latitude of 45°, and had suggested that from this unit the units of other categories could be derived.[10]

Following these earlier attempts and suggestions, Beccaria now came out in his report with a clear and comprehensive plan; however, he was not proposing it for adoption in the near future because, he said, people are always reluctant to accept radical changes of existing systems. And here is the description of Beccaria's plan, in the preparation of which, we are told, his friend Paolo Frisi played an important part. First of all, Beccaria proposes the complete acceptance for his plan of the decimal system: all measures, he says, shall be divided in decimal fractions in view of the great simplicity that this type of arithmetic brings to all sorts of operations, including those dealing with physical phenomena and the most complex surface measurements.

It is necessary to start with the choice of a unit of length, and Beccaria describes how his colleague Paolo Frisi has suggested a unit derived from geodetic measurements. For this purpose Frisi has proposed to select as the new mile a measure having the length of a minute of latitude in the parallel of Milan. The new unit of length would be a fraction of the new mile and would be divided into $\frac{1}{10}$, $\frac{1}{100}$, $\frac{1}{1,000}$ to form smaller measures, while longer measures would be obtained by multiplying it by 10, 100, 1,000. Since the measures of length would be based on terrestrial dimensions, they would be linked also to the surface measures; and this connection, explains Beccaria, would enable us to have very accurate maps.

From these standards Beccaria then develops his system by entering the other categories of measures and weights, always on the basis of the fundamental unit of length. The standard of weight could be obtained by making a cube of a homogeneous matter, such as a noble metal; this cube would be related to the unit of length by the fact that its side would have that measure or a decimal part of it, and the weight of the cube would be the new unit of weight. A standard of capacity should be chosen with the same procedure, and, like all other standards, it would be divided and multiplied in decimals. In this way, says Beccaria, we would have the great advantage of having

---

10. Simon Stevin, or Stevinus (1548–1620), Dutch mathematician; in 1586 he published a small pamphlet dealing with decimal fractions; he also published *Statics and Hydrostatics*.

Jean Picard (1620–82), French astronomer; he provided the first accurate measure of a degree of a meridian, thus enabling Newton to verify his theory of gravitation.

the whole system of weights and measures connected with a measure of length based on the terrestrial size, and all our arithmetic would be freed from complicated fractions. Besides, if by chance we should lose all the main standards of length, weight, and capacity, in order to remake them we would need only to keep the memory of this system, so simple that a few lines would describe it. This is a plan, Beccaria makes clear, that he does not submit for serious consideration because its features are too far from the present reality; and we should remember, he concludes, that often the greatest enemy of good is the search for something better.

And so Beccaria, having made his practical proposals for limited solutions in Lombardy, presented his great world plan only as a distant goal, a dream to be realized if and when the times would be mature for it. He could not know then that the realization of this dream was not far off. Ten years later, in 1790, in the climate of reform that was brought about by the French Revolution, Charles de Talleyrand presented to the French National Assembly a report in which a universal system of measures was advocated.[11]

The assembly appointed a committee to consider the suitability of adopting a fraction of the meridian as the new length unit; and when this committee proposed to choose as the new unit of length the meter, that is a 1/40,000,000 part of the terrestrial meridian, a commission was appointed to draw up a whole system of weights and measures, all based on the meter as the fundamental unit and on the decimal scale for all their multiples and fractions. Thus, a decimal system was developed in which the square meter, the liter, and the kilogram became the units in their categories, all being based on the meter as the unit of length. In 1799 a law established the new standards officially; the new system became compulsory in France in 1801, and soon after in many other countries. Beccaria was dead by then, but his dream of a universal system of weights and measures had come true: a system almost identical in principle to the one he had first outlined, with all the standards interrelated and based on a unit of length derived from the terrestrial circumference, the whole system made simple by the adoption of the decimal scale.

---

11. Charles Maurice de Talleyrand-Périgord (1754–1838) was a member of the French National Assembly; he took part in the revolutionary movement and later became the French foreign minister who represented his country at the Congress of Vienna after Napoleon's defeat.

A Period of

Enlightened Reforms

T HE French commission which years later unified on a decimal basis all the standards of weights and measures certainly was acquainted with Beccaria's early suggestions. His proposals had been made public long before the commission began to work on its assignment; moreover, some of the members, Condorcet and Lagrange especially, seem to have been in direct contact—if not with Beccaria himself—with Paolo Frisi or some of their mutual friends. To whom, then, should go the credit for the realization of this important undertaking? The Frenchman Collin de Plancy, writing fairly soon after the adoption of the new system, gave Beccaria the credit for the great innovation: "We should not forget that he had the glory of proposing to his government, already in 1781, the decimal system of weights and measures that the Revolution has since adopted in France." Years later, the Italian Cesare Cantù was no less chivalrous than Collin de Plancy when he said that Beccaria with the help of Frisi had indeed presented the first plan long before the French gave that suggestion a practical effect; but, said Cantù: "We proposed it and they did it, an important difference that we should not minimize." This is surely a rare example of two writers trying to give a fair judgment in an area in which nationalistic bias so often prevails.[1]

In Vienna the government gave great importance to the problem of unification of the standards of weights and measures. Although Beccaria's suggestions for a universal system were considered much too daring for the time, full support was given to his limited plan for Lombardy, and at the end of 1781 the government asked him to give an account of what had been accomplished so far. Beccaria reported that there was by then only one unit of length in the whole of Lombardy, but that the unification of the other units was still being worked out. In his report Beccaria explained, among other things, the difficulty of making with a solid matter a standard of weight that would be related to the unit of length. But, continued Beccaria, there is another method of establishing the link between length and weight: through the unit of capacity. By making a cubic vase having the unit of length as its side, wrote Beccaria, "we can then fill it with water, distilled several times in order to assure its homogeneity; and by weighing the water contained in the vase we will have the units of length, weight, and capacity, all related to one another." This very method was used later by the French scientists when they put these ideas on a practical plane.[2]

The minister in charge of Italian affairs in Vienna, Baron Sperges, followed Beccaria's reports closely and often praised him for his work. This was a period of intense activity for Beccaria. He not only continued to handle the problem of food supplies for the city of Milan, but between 1780 and 1783 he prepared many studies on a variety of subjects: the trade between Lombardy and Switzerland, the new regulations concerning the Milan bakeries, the production of the iron mines, the state of pastures and forests in Lombardy. As regards these last subjects, we see again Beccaria's preoccupation with the conservation of natural resources in his proposals for better controls and new laws having as their object the care of forests and mines.

---

1. See Beccaria, *Des délits et des peines,* ed. Collin de Plancy, p. xxv, and Cantù, p. 340. (Collin de Plancy erroneously mentioned 1781 as the year in which Beccaria presented his plan on the unification of weights and measures; it was, to be exact, 1780.)

For the relations of French scientists with Milanese correspondents see Landry, pp. 15–16n. Only one letter of Condorcet to Beccaria, written in 1771, has been preserved (see Landry, pp. 178–80).

2. For Beccaria's report of 1781 on the standard of weight and his proposal to establish the link between length and weight through the unit of capacity see Cantù, pp. 339–40.

The empress Maria Theresa had died in 1780 after a long reign. The new emperor, Joseph II, was eager to continue his mother's reforms in many fields. Although in certain matters he was considered too autocratic, on the whole he had a liberal mind and soon after his accession to the throne he gave proof of it when, in 1781, he promoted an Act of Tolerance by which the Jews and other non-Catholics were freed from the restrictions that had previously been imposed on them. Maria Theresa, with all her good qualities, had not been blameless in this respect.

Economic Reforms

In Milan the economic council continued to do its work and Beccaria was, as usual, one of its most active members. Especially noteworthy for the advanced social ideas expressed in it is a report that he wrote in 1784 on the organization of medical services in the Lombard countryside. A large part of this report is taken up by details on the location of medical centers and country doctors, and by suggestions aimed at covering more fully the needs of the inhabitants, especially in sparsely populated areas. But one of the problems for which Beccaria shows particular concern is medical care for the poor. In the past some religious institutions had provided services to poor people, but now the whole medical system was coming gradually under governmental jurisdiction and it was becoming necessary to guarantee full medical care to all people, both rich and poor. To this end Beccaria proposes in his report that a government subsidy be granted to country doctors, so that they may keep their fees at a minimum and thus enable even people of modest means to afford them. This subsidy, Beccaria advises, should also make it possible for the doctors to serve the poor without any charge. The problem arises, however, of determining who is to be considered poor, and Beccaria admits that it is not easy to identify those who would really deserve gratuitous service. We know, he says, that there are people who pretend to be poor, people who want to be poor, and those who are poor because they spend what they have in bad habits. Beccaria's answer is simple: in case of illness, the law of humanity and a wise policy oblige us to help all these people, if not as individuals, as members of mankind. Almost all the peasants, says Beccaria, would probably qualify as poor, but it would not be right to extend gratuitous service automatically to all of them because some are, nevertheless, a little better off than others; and it would be unfair to ask the doctors to serve them all without charge in view of the modesty of their subsidy. Beccaria adds that, not having all the data, he is unable to give an exact estimate of the number of people who may be entitled to gratuitous service; he advises, therefore, that, pending a more complete survey, the amount appropriated for this project be left flexible.

In his report Beccaria finally expresses his satisfaction with the plan, already announced by the government, to increase from thirteen to thirty-four the number of hospitals in the Lombard countryside; and here, too, he stresses the necessity of free hospitalization for the poor, as well as the free supply of drugs and medicines. This is another example of Beccaria's social conscience; his sensitive reaction to the needs and aspirations of the masses foreshadowed a policy which would gradually be adopted in many civilized countries.

Around this time, or soon after, Beccaria presented several other interesting reports, among them a new, detailed study on the trade with Switzerland, with proposals for changes in the existing treaties in order to reach a fair balance between imports and exports; and he also submitted a report concerning the organization of chambers of commerce in several Lombard cities.

In 1785 the emperor Joseph II made a tour of the empire, including Lombardy, as a result of which the economic council was replaced in Milan by the Imperial Government Council with greater authority and responsibilities. The new council had seven departments, and Beccaria was appointed head of the third, the very important Department of Agriculture, Industry and Commerce. This appointment confirmed the high esteem in which Beccaria was held and did credit to a government that appreciated and encouraged the best men who served it.

If Beccaria was gaining satisfaction in his public career, not everything was perfect in his private life. It is true that his second marriage was working well, that Anna was a very good wife, and that their son, Giulio, was a friendly little boy, very attached to his father. "He is good and intelligent," wrote Pietro Verri of young Giulio, "he resembles his father." Indeed times had changed. However, there were also troubles. Beccaria's sister, Maddalena, had been left a widow after only two years of marriage and had married again. She decided now to sue her brother Cesare because at the time of her first marriage she had renounced some trust money from an old inheritance to which, on second thought, she felt she had some right. The matter was obviously far from clear, for the suit lasted a long time and an appeal was still pending many years later. This was the first legal trouble that Beccaria was to have with members of his family.

In 1782 his father had died at the age of eighty-five, leaving an estate that included the house on Via Brera, the country place in Gessate, and other assets valued at about 60,000 lire. Cesare, being the firstborn son, received the largest part of the inheritance.[3]

In the meantime Beccaria's older daughter, Giulia, had left the monastery of San Paolo and had come to live at home with the rest of the family. Her father found that she had acquired from the nuns some "unreasonable ideas." Pietro Verri commented that Beccaria, on the contrary, should have been happy that she was a sensible and well-balanced woman in spite of the internment. She was now twenty, and a middle-aged widower, Pietro Manzoni, was showing interest in her. This Manzoni, forty-six years of age, was not too brilliant, but was cultivated and of good family; and Beccaria pushed his daughter into an engagement that was not very wise. She was young, however, just out of a nuns' school, and she raised no objection.

At that time—it was the summer of 1782—Cesare took his wife and little Giulio to Genoa on a pleasure trip, and soon after their return Giulia's wedding took place. It was to be an unhappy marriage: Giulia was exuberant and enjoyed society life, as her mother had, while her husband, twenty-six years her elder, preferred a quiet and retired life. The result was that Giulia was often in good company without her husband who became jealous and suspicious. Three years after the marriage a son was born, Alessandro, who was to become one of Italy's greatest writers, author of the classic novel *I Promessi Sposi*. Few believe that Pietro Manzoni was his father. With the birth of Alessandro, Beccaria became a grandfather at the age of forty-seven.

His new position as the head of the important third department in the imperial council kept Beccaria busier than ever, as shown by the report on the department's first year of activity that he presented in

---

3. Except for the real estate properties, the assets left by Beccaria's father were rather modest and they could not easily be converted into cash. As regards the value of the lira, it took about twenty lire to make an English pound (or five lire to make a dollar when the American currency was established).

February of 1787. Beccaria's report gave a detailed account of what had already been done and what was planned for the future in all the fields that fell under the department's jurisdiction, including such matters as food supplies, chambers of commerce, coinage, fairs and markets, weights and measures, mines, fishing and hunting, population statistics. All these matters, and many others, had been assigned to the Department of Agriculture, Industry and Commerce. A brief summary of this report will show how eager Beccaria was to see a further expansion of all the economic and cultural activities of Lombardy.

First of all, this report is noteworthy because we see that Beccaria's adherence to the physiocratic doctrine of laissez faire, never complete to be sure, had weakened during his years in the government. He now seemed more and more convinced that the function of the government as a regulating agent was necessary, and he expressed the view that the government's playing a larger role in several fields might be beneficial. No doubt, the efficiency and basic honesty of the Austrian administration contributed to Beccaria's acceptance of this concept.

One of the subjects discussed by Beccaria in his report was the production of silk, the most important industry of Lombardy. In recent years there had been an increase in the output of silk, and Beccaria ascribed this increase to a higher duty imposed by the central government on the importation of foreign silk and to special measures favoring the marketing of Lombard silk throughout the empire. The success of this policy, said Beccaria, shows that it is always better to encourage some industry or activity by general and not individual measures. In fact, Beccaria had opposed the granting of subsidies to some of the manufacturers because in his view such a policy would have favored unjustly a few industrialists and would have created an unhealthy precedent, contrary to the best economic principles.

Another interesting point in Beccaria's report is the one dealing with the granting of prizes to workers and farmers who had increased their output or had adopted new implements or systems of production. Such an initiative had been suggested by Beccaria in his course at the Palatine School and now he was able to put it into effect and see its usefulness in real life. In the report Beccaria gives the details of the awards and also speaks of the Patriotic Society, a new foundation offering prizes to the authors of essays outlining improvements in the fields of industry and agriculture. These accomplishments were undoubtedly of great satisfaction to Beccaria who, in his course, had spoken of these projects without really expecting that they would be soon realized.

As regards the subject of weights and measures, Beccaria notes with pleasure that the unification of the measure of length in the whole of Lombardy has worked out very successfully, but he admits that some problems are still unsolved as far as the other standards are concerned. Once more he points out the great advantage that the choice of a minute of latitude as the length of the new mile would have as a basis for an overall solution in this field; but he does not insist on it and again he stresses the necessity of making these changes gradually in order to avoid difficulties and confusion in economic and commercial activities.

As regards the iron mines and the foundries, Beccaria is pleased to report an increase in their output and in their production of finished metal—not only regular iron, but also steel, which had never before been manufactured in Lombardy. Beccaria's proposals for sending some local young men to study the operations in other parts of the empire had been accepted and the first students had just been employed in the Lombard mines after a period of training in the mines of Styria and Carinthia: another case in which Beccaria was able to put his theoretical ideas to a practical test.

Among the other statements contained in this report we find some interesting observations concerning hunting rules. Beccaria advocates strict laws governing hunting activities and the granting of hunting licenses; in his view a firm policy in this field would be justified by the harm done by the indiscriminate destruction of wild animals. But the granting of hunting licenses, says Beccaria, should be the object of great care for still another reason: public security. This may mean a restriction of personal freedom, but Beccaria thinks that it is in the general interest to accept this limitation. A hunting license, explains Beccaria, means permission to go around armed, either individually or in groups; it is clear, therefore, that such permission should not be granted to everyone, but should be given, within certain bounds and controls, only to qualified persons who would not endanger public security and tranquillity.

Finally, to mention one more interesting proposal in the report— that concerning the population of the region—Beccaria notes that the existing statistics do not show anything except the number of inhabitants, and of births, deaths, and marriages. It is, of course, useful to know how a population has increased or decreased in a province; but, says Beccaria, figures become really valuable when they enable us to take measures to improve certain conditions, especially those connected with public health and security. For this reason Beccaria suggests that in the future the population surveys be much more detailed and include personal data, such as trends of specific illnesses and other facts that may be of value for the well-being of the people.

Soon after the presentation of this important report on the initial activity of his department of the imperial council, Beccaria submitted several other studies on matters entrusted to him. Around this time he wrote reports on his inspection of the silk and wool industries in the zone of Como, on measures necessary to stop the smuggling of foreign silk and other textile products into Lombardy, and on the problem of unemployment which was troubling the silk industry despite the increase in production. Other studies concerned taxation, loans to industries, forest conservation, trade between Lombardy and the German provinces of the empire, cultivation of rice, and labor relations. This last subject was beginning to become an important problem with the development of large mechanized factories employing a vast number of workers.[4]

As regards the trade between Lombardy and the German provinces of the Austrian empire, it is interesting to note that a point under discussion was the route to be followed between the two territories. Of course, means of transportation were still primitive, since steamers and trains had not yet made their appearance. The alternative routes were the roads through the Tyrolean Alps or the waterway (along the river Po and across the Adriatic) to the port of Trieste and from there the land route to the north. Despite the hardships of the Tyrol route during the winter season, it gradually became the favored one because it was shorter and less expensive.[5]

---

4. Two newly found notes of Beccaria on problems connected with the cultivation of rice in Lombardy were published by Rosalba Canetta in 1971 (see bibliography).

5. The documents dealing with the trade between Lombardy and the German provinces of the empire were drawn up under the supervision of Beccaria, who annotated them in his own hand. I wish to thank Professor Romani of the Catholic University of Milan for sending photostats of these documents.

The Veterinary School

A task that seems to have fascinated Beccaria in that period was the organization of the first veterinary school in Lombardy. The opening of such a school had been authorized by the government and the preparation of plans for its establishment fell under the jurisdiction of Beccaria's department. This was not a simple undertaking because the scientific teaching of veterinary medicine was quite new at that time and Beccaria could not have much help from the example of other schools.

The first part of the eighteenth century was certainly not an enlightened age as far as veterinary science is concerned. In all European countries and in their colonies the care of animals was in the hands of farriers, men who combined the art of horseshoeing with veterinary treatment and surgery. As a rule, these farriers had little general education, but they learned how to cope with the most common diseases of horses and cattle. Relatively speaking, all was well as long as there were no widespread cases of complicated diseases or epidemics among animals. But the danger in this inadequate system became evident when it was realized that from 1710 to 1760 about 200 million cattle died in Europe of rinderpest, the so-called cattle plague.

One may also imagine the many medicines and remedies that were offered by quacks to make the animals stronger and healthier. The following advertisement, from the *New York Gazette* of August 22, 1765, seems especially picturesque:

> Notice to the Publick—That Augustus Stewart of New Jersey has prepared a HORSE POWDER, which for its qualities and operations exceeds any thing hitherto contrived for the benefit of that animal. In all disorders to which those creatures are liable, it gives quick relief, purifies the blood, makes the beast more than ordinary lively, brisk, and strong, and occasions him to thrive in fatness, on almost half the provisions he in common devours. It is a great preservative against disorders of all kinds, giving only one common tablespoon full of it once a week.[6]

It was a Frenchman, Claude Bourgelat, who not only saw the necessity of raising veterinary education to the college level, but actu-

---

6. Quoted from G. C. Christensen, "Genesis of Veterinary Education in the United States," *Journal of the American Veterinary Medical Association,* vol. 128, no. 9 (Chicago, 1956), pp. 437–40.

ally organized the first veterinary school in the city of Lyons in 1761. A second school was opened in France, at Alfort, in 1765. The French example was soon followed in other countries and veterinary schools were established in Turin, Vienna, and some other cities of continental Europe. These schools were newly formed and still in a tentative stage when Beccaria was asked to organize the school of Milan. Consequently, he had to face and solve many problems, and it took several years to lay the groundwork for such a project.

The decision to open a veterinary school was opposed strongly by the Lombard farriers, who saw their livelihood threatened by the future appearance of young graduates ready to take over the care of animals. Therefore, Beccaria had to proceed with a certain diplomacy in his plan, promising the old farriers that they would not lose their jobs if they were already well-established and could give proof of their experience. For the future, however, there could be no compromise: the establishment of the new school, said Beccaria, was an essential step taken in the interest of the state economy.

In normal times the Lombard farriers had, on the whole, done good work, but Beccaria did not hesitate to declare, in a report describing his plan for the new school, that in times of epidemics the farriers' interventions had proved not only inadequate but actually harmful, with bad consequences to agriculture and other activities. With the opening of the new school, said Beccaria, the danger of such crises would be eliminated.[7]

As was already said, Beccaria had to solve many problems: he had, first, to propose a suitable location for the school, and then to see how to organize the instruction courses, how to appoint the teachers, how to choose the books, and how to make all the financial arrangements connected with the school's operation. Having the option of choosing a location in Milan or in some other town in Lombardy, Beccaria designated Milan as the best place for the new school and proposed to install it in an unused hospital, the *Lazzaretto,* a building large enough to provide free lodgings for the students coming to Milan from other towns.

As for the teaching, Beccaria proposed two different courses of instruction: a scientific course of four years for those who wanted to

---

7. Beccaria's plan for the veterinary school of Milan is described in Beccaria, *Opere,* ed. Romagnoli, vol. 2, pp. 531–54.

become veterinarians, either in public administration or as private practitioners, and an elementary course of only one year for those who wanted to become licensed farriers, authorized to take care of simple and common illnesses. As regards the higher course, Beccaria made clear that the instruction in a veterinary school had to be as serious and complete as that of a medical school; in fact, he said, there is no difference between the two sciences except for the object on which they are applied; therefore, the requirements for admission to this higher course should be similar to those of other graduate studies. As to the elementary course of one year, Beccaria stated that this would be, from then on, a necessary instruction for those who wanted to become regular farriers. For the admission to this limited course the requirements were kept low enough so that people with an elementary education would be accepted. In any case, the time of the self-educated farrier was definitely over.

Beccaria's plan was approved by the government in 1789 and Milan thus became one of the first cities in the world to have a veterinary school. Soon after, veterinary schools were established in England and, many years later, in the United States and Canada.[8]

The First Labor Troubles in Lombardy

In 1789 the imperial council of Milan underwent some changes in its organization, and Beccaria, who was now fifty-one, was made the head of the second department, which had jurisdiction over matters connected with public security, including the penal code, the police, the courts of justice, the prisons, and the houses of correction. From Paris had come the news that the populace had stormed the Bastille

---

8. The first veterinary school in England was that of London, established soon after the one in Milan, in 1791; Edinburgh followed in 1823. Strangely enough, the United States was very slow in establishing regular veterinary schools despite the large number of cattle and horses in the country; undoubtedly the lack of proper treatment was responsible for great losses of animals in the first part of the nineteenth century. The first legal veterinary schools in the United States were set up between 1850 and 1860 in Philadelphia, Boston, and New York; in 1879 Iowa State University was the first state-supported university to open a department of veterinary medicine. In Canada the first veterinary schools were those of Toronto and Montreal, established in 1862 and 1866.

For more details about the development of veterinary schools in Italy and other countries see *Le facoltà scientifiche* (Bologna: Il Mulino, 1964), pp. 249 ff.; for the United States see the article by G. C. Christensen mentioned in n. 6 above.

on July 14, but Lombardy still seemed like a peaceful place far from the hurricane, and a wave of unrest among the textile workers of Como was dismissed as an isolated incident. In fact, the whole Austrian empire, having enacted so many beneficial reforms in the last fifty years, seemed safe from any violence or disorder.

Forty years under Maria Theresa and almost ten years under Joseph II had indeed brought about many changes for the better: the economy of the whole empire had been stimulated by great public works, commerce and industry had been promoted, maritime activities had been encouraged and the town of Trieste on the Adriatic was being developed into a major port, the customs system had been reorganized, the codes had been unified, the estates of the Church and the nobles had been submitted to regular taxation, various other Church privileges had been curtailed, and the whole fiscal system had been made more equitable.

As regards Lombardy in particular, the list is certainly impressive. First of all, there were the reforms concerning old Church customs and privileges: the right of asylum had been abolished, as had the Inquisition and the private jails of religious communities, the clergy had been brought under the jurisdiction of the government courts, ecclesiastical censorship had been repealed, the burial of the dead in churches had been prohibited, and suburban cemeteries had been established. The prohibition of church burial had been strongly opposed by the religious orders: Pietro Verri relates that in some convents the nuns sewed up the clothes of their dead sisters and stiffened the material with tar, so that the morticians who came to take them away would not be able to see their bodies. Among other important accomplishments we must mention the monetary reform, the new regulations concerning the standards of weights and measures, the construction of new roads and canals, the new rules regarding medical centers and country doctors, the construction of many new hospitals, the establishment of public libraries, the reorganization of the University of Pavia and of the Palatine School of Milan, and the establishment in Milan of the Academy of Fine Arts and that of the new veterinary school.

Beccaria had contributed substantially to many of these innovations and perhaps for this reason he seemed convinced that there would be steady improvement in the future as in the past, and that all problems would be solved gradually with goodwill and hard work. He kept this optimism despite more personal adversities and disappointments. In 1788 his second daughter, Maria, who had always been rather frail, died at the age of twenty-one. Soon after, the older daughter, Giulia, sued her father for a larger part in Maria's inheritance on account of his second marriage which, in Giulia's view, made him lose the right to his share. Through her lawyer Giulia stated that all her misfortunes had been caused by her father, who had forced her, when she was only sixteen, to marry a man for whom she felt only aversion and repugnance. It is not clear how she could say that she was sixteen at the time of her marriage when, in fact, she was twenty. Not until after Beccaria's death would this suit be settled by his son Giulio.

The emperor Joseph II died in 1790 and was succeeded by his brother, Leopold II, who had been a liberal ruler as Grand Duke of Tuscany. Around this time Beccaria was entrusted by the government with a difficult and delicate assignment in connection with the problem of labor relations in the textile industry. The development of the silk industry in the Como area had been accompanied by growing tensions between the factory owners and the workers. Since there were no labor contracts, wages were lowered when work was scarce and men were dismissed without any compensation. The ups and downs of silk production meant a precarious existence for the workers and a constant fear of remaining without a job.

Beccaria had already investigated the problem when he was in charge of the third department of the imperial council. He had then proposed to the municipality of Como several measures, among them the granting of a subsidy to the unemployed. In Beccaria's view, since Como had benefited from the development of the silk industry, it was the city's duty to take care of its unemployed citizens. This idea was quite new and daring in the eighteenth century and the city council had received it with little enthusiasm. Beccaria had also suggested that a commission be appointed to study the possibility of attracting to Como some other industries of a different kind, since a city that bases its economy on only one industry is more subject to crises than is one with diversified activities.

Nothing of what Beccaria had suggested had been done. All this was now past history, and the situation had grown steadily worse until, in 1790, Como had its first wave of unrest: groups of workers demonstrated in the streets, there was some violence, the police had to intervene and a number of arrests was made. Beccaria was then asked to go to Como again in order to study the situation and propose measures to restore the peace and avoid similar occurrences in the future.

In his report, dated September 17, 1790, Beccaria made clear that in his opinion a policy of repression could only make the situation worse. Seeing that the workers' hardships were very real and that they were indeed at the mercy of the industrialists, he strongly opposed the proposal advanced by some prominent citizens of Como to round up the unruly workers and put them in the army. Whatever the infraction committed by any worker, said Beccaria, it falls under the jurisdiction of the judicial power; any other measure would be harmful and would create a new fear among the working people, who will simply wait for the first opportunity to emigrate.

Beccaria saw what he called "the odious and irritating contrast between the poverty of the pleading workers and the wealth of the citizens armed in defense against them." This sentence of Beccaria, often quoted, appeared as an early indictment against social injustice and reminds us that the labor forces started their fight for better conditions from a position of great weakness.

Beccaria's mission was undoubtedly very successful. His sympathy for the workers' plight and, at the same time, the tact he showed in his discussions with the industrialists, were of great help in creating a better atmosphere in the area. Looking still to a more distant future, he made some practical suggestions aimed at putting the whole economy of that zone on a sounder basis and among other proposals he once more urged the city council of Como to study the possibility of encouraging a diversification of local activities.

Beccaria had hardly begun his work in the new department of the imperial council when, early in 1791, he was also appointed a member of a commission for the reform of criminal legislation in Lombardy. Chancellor Kaunitz informed Beccaria that the emperor Leopold II himself had designated him as a first member of the commission, and asked Beccaria to suggest a small number of qualified persons who might be assigned to this project. The recently adopted Austrian code had not been extended to Lombardy in view of that province's different traditions. The commission for the new code, wrote Kaunitz, shall study the possibility of applying the Austrian code to Lombardy, but also will be able to choose freely from the old laws and from the code of Tuscany, taking into consideration the needs and conditions of the local population. The reference to the Tuscan code is noteworthy because the emperor Leopold II had prepared it himself when he had been Grand Duke of Tuscany, and in it he had followed many of the recommendations outlined by Beccaria in his treatise *On Crimes and Punishments*.

That little book, which had given Beccaria world fame twenty-five years before, in the meantime had had a tremendous impact in many countries, and it seemed only right that he should now participate in the reform of penal laws and contribute to the progress of justice in his own land.

10

The Growing Interest in Penal Legislation

Beccaria's treatise *On Crimes and Punishments* had aroused a deep interest in criminal legislation and had greatly influenced the attitudes of people and governments toward the administration of justice. While the treatise continued to appear in more and more editions in many languages, countless books and pamphlets were published everywhere having as their subject the criminal laws. Their authors were all eager to examine the weakness of the existing system and to discuss ways to correct it. No longer would Beccaria be able to say that "very few have sought to demolish the errors accumulated through the centuries in the penal codes." The discussions stimulated by all these publications put the criminal legislation in the forefront of current problems and contributed to the development of a widespread feeling that reforms were overdue and seriously needed. It is impossible to describe here all the publications that appeared in that period, but the brief review that follows will give an idea of how much attention was paid to the subject of penal laws in the wake of Beccaria's treatise.

In the Italian states many writers took an interest in the problem and generally supported Beccaria's principles, although a few of them, like Antonio Montanari and Franchino Rusca, disagreed with some of his views. Other authors—among them Paolo Risi, as well as Pietro Verri himself—wrote essays in which they discussed the use of torture and presented arguments for its abolition. In Rome Filippo Renazzi published three volumes in Latin (*Elementa juris criminalis*) in which he tried to present a first scientific elaboration of Beccaria's theories. But more important was the work of Gaetano Filangieri, the *Scienza della legislazione,* in which the author developed with intelligence and thoroughness Beccaria's principles, opposing him, however, on the question of the death penalty.[1]

Another upholder of the death penalty turned out to be Gian Rinaldo Carli who had endorsed many of Beccaria's theories, but could not accept the abolition of capital punishment. Carli's argument in favor of the death penalty was an unusual one. After pointing out that the right to kill a dangerous criminal in self-defense is inherent in human nature and is recognized by the laws of every country, Carli expressed the view that if the assaulted person is killed, "this right with all its attributes is transferred automatically to the public authority which is the protector and guarantor of the life of all citizens." Therefore, according to Carli, the right of self-defense—although stretched to a point where there is no real act of self-defense— entitles public authority to take the life of the culprit.[2]

In France Voltaire in his old age wrote several pamphlets supporting the basic ideas of Beccaria, but he hesitated to endorse the complete abolition of capital punishment. A stand in favor of penal reforms in line with Beccaria's theories was taken in 1766 by Michel

---

1. For a detailed account of Italian writings of that period on criminal problems see Cantù, pp. 181 ff.; also Maestro, pp. 127–28. For comments on Beccaria's treatise and excerpts from works of Italian writers see Beccaria, *Dei delitti e delle pene,* ed. Venturi, pp. 186 ff.

The first edition of Gaetano Filangieri's *Scienza della legislazione* was published in Naples as follows: vols. 1 and 2 in 1780, vols. 3 and 4 (dealing with criminal jurisprudence) in 1783, vols. 5, 6, and 7 in 1785. Vol. 8 (on laws concerning religion) appeared posthumously in 1791. Filangieri had planned also a vol. 9 of which he left only a brief outline. His *Scienza della legislazione* was reprinted many times and was translated into English and numerous other languages. The author's views on the necessity of reform in the Roman Catholic church aroused the enmity of the ecclesiastical authorities, and his work was placed on the Index of condemned books. Filangieri died in 1788, at the age of thirty-six.

2. See De Stefano, *G.R. Carli (1720–1795)—Contributo alla storia delle origini del Risorgimento italiano,* p. 48.

Servan, a jurist who questioned the legality of capital punishment. Another jurist, Louis Philippon de La Madelaine, delivered a speech in 1770 calling for ample reforms and the outright abolition of the death penalty. Other writings on many aspects of criminal legislation were published around that time by Brissot de Warville, Mirabeau, Lacretelle, Marat, Condorcet, and Linguet—and they all supported reforms in accordance with Beccaria's principles. While the party of the reformers was becoming stronger, the opposition to the new ideas by the most conservative jurists was now weak and confused.[3]

In Austria the great jurist Joseph von Sonnenfels, a professor of law at the University of Vienna, was much impressed by Beccaria's principles and decided to fight in his country for the abolition of torture and of the death penalty. When the empress Maria Theresa pointed out to him that his teachings contradicted some of the existing laws, he wrote her such an eloquent letter that she asked him to explain his theories more extensively. He then wrote a little book entitled *On the Abolition of Torture* (*Ueber die Abschaffung der Tortur,* 1775) which had a great success and was promptly translated into Italian.

Beccaria's treatise *On Crimes and Punishments* aroused a great interest in Germany. The first German translation by Albrecht Wittenberg, not too satisfactory since it was based on Morellet's French text, appeared in Hamburg as early as 1766. Another translation by Jakob Schultes, based on the original Italian, was published a year later in Ulm; but the most popular German edition of Beccaria's treatise was to be the one translated by Philip Jacob Flade and presented with a long introduction by Karl Ferdinand Hommel in 1778. Hommel was a well-known professor in Leipzig, and his unbounded admiration for Beccaria is shown by the title he gave to his edition of the treatise: *The Immortal Work of the Marquis Beccaria on Crimes and Punishments.* Because of his devotion to Beccaria's principles Hommel was later called by other jurists "the German Beccaria."[4]

The enthusiasm for Beccaria in Germany was not shared by every-

---

3. For a survey of Voltaire's contribution to the penal reforms see Maestro, pp. 100 ff. For details on other French authors and their writings on penal problems see Esmein, *Histoire de la procédure criminelle en France,* pp. 376 ff.; also Hertz, *Voltaire und die französische Strafrechtspflege im achtzehnten Jahrhundert,* pp. 449 ff.

4. For an Italian translation of Hommel's introduction to his edition of Beccaria's treatise see Beccaria, *Dei delitti e delle pene,* ed. Venturi, pp. 597–624.

body, and one of his most bitter critics was the famous philosopher Immanuel Kant, who was especially enraged by Beccaria's proposal to abolish the death penalty. Kant's stand in favor of capital punishment was based on his assumption that penal justice required punishments equal to the offenses. In his *Metaphysic of Morals* (*Metaphysik der Sitten*, published in 1797 but undoubtedly written sometime earlier) Kant accused Beccaria of affected humanitarianism and defined Beccaria's arguments against the death penalty as mere sophistry and perversion of true justice. Ignoring all the other reasons given by Beccaria for the abolition of the death penalty, Kant attacked Beccaria for having said that under the social contract no one would put his own life willingly in other people's hands. But no one—said Kant, twisting Beccaria's thought—is punished for having wanted the *punishment,* he is punished for having wanted *an action deserving punishment.* Having made this statement, Kant was apparently completely satisfied as to the rightfulness of the death penalty.[5]

A country where Beccaria's ideas found fertile ground was Poland, where the treatise *On Crimes and Punishments* was received with considerable interest soon after its publication. The treatise appeared in Polish in 1772, but prior to that year it had already circulated in its Italian and French editions. Several Polish jurists, among them Teodor Ostrowski, supported Beccaria's proposal to abolish the death penalty, advocating in its stead prison sentences with compulsory labor for the inmates in an atmosphere conducive to their rehabilitation. Poland was indeed one of the countries where the climate for reform appeared especially favorable, but unfortunately the projects for a new penal code were disrupted by the wars which in 1794 resulted in the end of Polish independence.[6]

Even in Spain, a country far behind the others in the reform movement, a few enlightened men succeeded in arousing some interest in the new ideas. Despite the power that the Inquisition still had in Spain, a translation of Beccaria's book by Juan Antonio de las Casas

---

5. See Kant, *Werke,* vol. 5: *Metaphysik der Sitten* (*Rechtslehre,* pp. 166 ff.; for Kant's attack on Beccaria see pp. 170 ff.). Mondolfo, an admirer of Kant, nevertheless criticized the German philosopher for his rigid attitude on this subject (Mondolfo, *Cesare Beccaria,* pp. 57 ff.).

6. For Beccaria's influence in Poland see the lecture by Prof. Stanislaw Plawski, "Cesare Beccaria et la politique pénitentiaire de Pologne," in *Accademia Nazionale dei Lincei—Problemi attuali di scienza e cultura, Quaderno no. 71,* pp. 61 ff.

appeared in 1774 thanks to the personal intervention of the minister Pedro Rodriguez de Campomanes. However, the climate that still prevailed in the country is clearly shown by the following note that the translator deemed necessary to print in his presentation of the book: "Should the doctrine contained in this treatise not be in complete conformity with the sentiments of our Holy Mother Church and the supreme rights of H.M., then, in that case, we are ready to detest such doctrine with the utmost submission and respect, since it is our duty to obey and to conform our judgment to that of our Teachers and Superiors."

The Inquisition in Madrid would not give up so easily: three years later, in 1777, the Spanish edition of Beccaria's book was condemned and its distribution was prohibited. Some courageous men, however, continued to fight despite all the dangers and hardships, and in 1782 Manuel de Lardizabal published a pamphlet in favor of penal reforms, thus showing that the fight had not been abandoned.[7]

In England the interest in criminal legislation grew considerably during those years and the need for reforms was felt by a growing number of people. It is true that England had developed a much better procedure than any other country and that the use of torture was illegal; but a shocking disproportion still existed between crimes and punishments, and penalties were often cruel and extremely severe. The first translator of Beccaria's treatise in his own preface to that early edition made the "melancholy reflection" that the number of criminals put to death in England was "much greater than in any other part of Europe."

Already in 1765 a moderate criticism of the English laws appeared in William Blackstone's *Commentaries on the Laws of England*. In his book Blackstone referred to the criminal laws of other countries and said that their inhumanity and mistaken policy had already been pointed out by writers such as Montesquieu and Beccaria. "But even with us in England," continued Blackstone, "where our crown law is with justice supposed to be more nearly advanced to perfection; where crimes are more accurately defined and penalties less uncertain and arbitrary; where all our accusations are public, and our trials in

---

7. For the title of Lardizabal's pamphlet see bibliography. For more details about Beccaria's influence in Spain see Beccaria, *Dei delitti e delle pene,* ed. Venturi, p. xxxii and pp. 564–71.

the face of the world; where torture is unknown, and every delin-
quent is judged by such of his equals against whom he can form no
exception nor even a personal dislike; even here we shall occasionally find room to remark some particulars that seem to want revision
and amendment."[8]

Blackstone seemed on the whole fairly satisfied with the existing
English law and he did not object to such corporal punishments as
the cutting off of the nose and ears. Apparently, these penalties were
not among the "particulars that seem to want revision and amendment." Still Blackstone was the first author in England to give distinct
treatment to criminal legislation and he did follow Beccaria in some
of his most progressive ideas and principles. In fact, according to Sir
William Holdsworth, "it was Beccaria's book which helped Blackstone
to crystallize his ideas, and it was Beccaria's influence which helped
to give a more critical tone to his treatment of the English criminal
law than to his treatment of any other part of English law."[9]

Among the prominent men who took an interest in criminal laws
was Oliver Goldsmith who, while in favor of capital punishment for
those guilty of murder, declared in 1766 that the death penalty
should not be applied against those who stole property. In the same
year the Scottish painter Allan Ramsay commented at length on Beccaria's treatise in a letter addressed to his friend Diderot. Although
skeptical about the possibility of any real change in the existing laws,
Ramsay had only praise for the good intentions and high ideals of
the Milanese reformer.[10]

A young jurist, Jeremy Bentham, began to be active at this time
and was soon to show his enthusiasm and dedication in the battle
for reforms. Bentham did not hesitate to criticize Blackstone for his
cautious approach, asserting that Blackstone's fundamental fault was
his "antipathy to reform"—an accusation that was not completely
justified. But surely there was no such antipathy in Bentham, a great
admirer of Beccaria who was all in favor of changes in the English

---

8. For the complete passage see Blackstone, *Commentaries on the Laws of
England,* book 4, chap. i, pp. 1426 ff.

9. For Beccaria's influence on Blackstone see Leon Radzinowicz, *A History
of English Criminal Law and its Administration from 1750—The Movement
for Reform 1750–1833,* pp. 345–46 (text and notes, including quoted statement
by Sir William Holdsworth).

10. For the text of Ramsay's letter to Diderot see Beccaria, *Dei delitti e
delle pene,* ed. Venturi, pp. 536–45.

penal system. Bentham was a disciple of Beccaria as well as of Helvétius, to whom Beccaria himself was indebted for some philosophical principles. In one of his writings Bentham could not refrain from addressing Beccaria as follows: "Oh, my master, first evangelist of reason, you who have raised your Italy so far above England, and I would add above France, were it not that Helvétius, without writing on the subject of laws, had already assisted you and had provided you with your fundamental ideas . . . you who have made so many useful excursions into the path of utility, what is there left for us to do?—Never to turn aside from that path."[11]

In his juridical essays Bentham made clear that Beccaria was the principal source of his penal theories, and this acknowledgment is also found in several of his letters, notably one addressed to Voltaire and another written to the Reverend John Forster.[12]

Both Bentham and, later, Samuel Romilly fought hard for a humane legislation, and they especially condemned the ease with which the death penalty was inflicted for common thefts. A stand against the disproportion between crimes and punishments was also taken by Sir William Meredith and William Eden, while John Howard started a movement for the improvement of prisons and criminal institutions. But there were other English writers who did not seem to care about the cruelty in their country's system. In 1784 Martin Madan protested against the frequency of pardons, adopting Beccaria's theory of the certainty of punishments as the best check on crime. His book, *Thoughts on Executive Justice,* had a strong influ-

---

11. See Elie Halévy, *The Growth of Philosophical Radicalism,* p. 21 (passage quoted from manuscript no. 32, University College Collection, London).

12. Beccaria's inspirational role is evident in Bentham's *Introduction to the Principles of Morals and Legislation.* See also *A Bentham Reader,* pp. 293–94 (essay "On the Art of Invention").

For Bentham's letters to Voltaire and Forster see *The Correspondence of Jeremy Bentham,* ed. Sprigge, vol. 1, p. 367, and vol. 2, p. 99. According to Sprigge, the letter to Voltaire, dated tentatively November 1776, was probably never sent. In it Bentham referred to Beccaria in Latin as his *lucerna.*

For Beccaria's influence on Bentham see Bowle, *Politics and Opinion in the Nineteenth Century—An Historical Introduction,* pp. 56–57, and the essay by H.L.A. Hart, "Beccaria and Bentham," in *Accademia delle Scienze di Torino, Atti del Convegno internazionale su Cesare Beccaria, Memorie—Classe di scienze morali, serie IV, no. 9.* For a study of wider scope see Phillipson, *Three Criminal Law Reformers: Beccaria, Bentham, Romilly;* Phillipson's book appraises Beccaria's influence and shows how the two English reformers, following Beccaria's principles, helped to change the criminal legislation of their country.

ence and the granting of pardons was severely reduced. However, Beccaria had opposed pardons in a system of mild laws, whereas mildness was not at all the rule in England at that time, so that after the publication of Madan's book one could often see the spectacle of ten or twenty criminals hanged one near the other. At the same time Archdeacon William Paley did his best to slow up the reform movement and to delay the enactment of the milder laws sponsored by Bentham and Romilly. In his book, *Moral and Political Philosophy,* published in 1785, he defended in the name of social utility the application of the capital penalty in almost all instances foreseen in the English law.[13]

Benjamin Franklin, who was then living in Europe as American minister to France, spoke often of the cruelty and absurdities in the existing legal systems. Being interested in almost every aspect of human life, Franklin could not be indifferent to the way justice was administered. When his friend Gaetano Filangieri sent him from Naples the first two volumes of his *Scienza della legislazione,* Franklin was happy to learn that the next volumes, dealing with criminal laws, were about to appear, and he wrote to Filangieri on January 11, 1783:

> The first two volumes of your excellent work, which were put into my hands by M. Pio, I perused with great pleasure. They are also much esteemed by some very judicious persons to whom I have lent them. . . . I was glad to learn that you were proceeding to consider the criminal laws, none have more need of reformation. They are everywhere in so great disorder, and so much injustice is committed in the execution of them, that I have been sometimes inclined to imagine less would exist in the world if there were no such laws, and the punishment of injuries were left to private resentment. I am glad, therefore, that you have not suffered yourself to be discouraged by any objections or apprehensions, and that we may soon expect the satisfaction of seeing two volumes on that subject which you have now under the press.[14]

---

13. A comprehensive coverage of writings by English jurists (with a good description of the reform movement in England) is given in Radzinowicz, *A History of English Criminal Law and its Administration from 1750—The Movement for Reform 1750–1833.* See also, by the same author, the article "Cesare Beccaria and the English System of Criminal Justice: A Reciprocal Relationship" (in the above mentioned publication of *Accademia delle Scienze di Torino*—see n. 12).

14. For the complete text of Franklin's letter to Filangieri see *The Writings of Benjamin Franklin,* ed. Smyth, vol. 9, pp. 1–3. M. Pio, mentioned in Franklin's letter to Filangieri, was chargé d'affaires of the court of Naples in Paris.

Some time later Franklin wrote a paper "On the criminal laws and the practice of privateering" which was presented in the form of a letter to Benjamin Vaughan dated March 14, 1785. This letter first appeared anonymously in a small volume entitled *Observations* that Samuel Romilly wrote as a refutation to the book by Martin Madan that we have already mentioned, *Thoughts on Executive Justice.* In his letter Franklin discussed the aspect of the English law that seemed to him most reprehensible, the disproportion between offenses and punishments. He wrote:

> If we really believe, as we profess to believe, that the law of Moses was the law of God, the dictate of divine wisdom, infinitely superior to human; on what principles do we ordain death as the punishment of an offence which, according to that law, was only to be punished by a restitution of fourfold? To put a man to death for an offence which does not deserve death, is it not murder?
>
> I see in the last newspaper from London that a woman is capitally convicted at the Old Bailey for privately stealing out of a shop some gauze, value fourteen shillings and threepence; is there any proportion between the injury done by the theft, value 14/3, and the punishment of a human creature, by death, on a gibbet? Might not that woman, by her labour, have made reparation ordained by God, in paying fourfold? Is not all punishment inflicted beyond the merit of the offence, so much punishment of innocence? In this light, how vast is the annual quantity of not only *injured*, but *suffering* innocence, in almost all the civilized states of Europe!
>
> If I think it right that the crime of murder should be punished with death, not only as an equal punishment of the crime, but to prevent other murders, does it follow that I must approve of inflicting the same punishment for a little invasion of my property by theft? If I am not myself so barbarous, so bloody-minded and revengeful, as to kill a fellow-creature for stealing from me 14/3, how can I approve of a law that does it?[15]

Franklin did not follow Beccaria in his opposition to the death penalty as a question of principle, but he shared the view that crime flourishes in a climate of cruelty and violence. In the same letter to Benjamin Vaughan, referring to the "late war of rapine and pillage" of England upon Holland and to the arming by the English government of hundreds of pirate vessels, Franklin asked: "After employing

15. For the full text of this letter see *The Writings of Benjamin Franklin,* ed. Smyth, vol. 9, pp. 291–99.

your people in robbing the Dutch, is it strange that, being put out of that employ by the peace, they should still continue robbing, and rob one another? . . . How can a nation whose government encouraged robbery have the face to condemn the crime in individuals?"

Other interesting writings on criminal legislation appeared in the last decades of the eighteenth century in the United States of America. These writings were closely connected with the actual reforms that were being enacted in the new republic and we will speak of them when describing penal reforms in the American states.

The activity of so many writers was the result of the interest that public opinion now took in the problems of criminal law. Reforms were demanded by more and more people, and even the traditional bodies of magistrates were now open to the new ideas. The time was ripe and reforms were enacted, one after another, in all countries. It would be unfair toward many other enlightened men to say that all this movement was the result of Beccaria's treatise, but that book was undoubtedly the one which had had the greatest influence and had given the reform movement that sense of urgency that was now felt everywhere.[16]

The first important reforms took place in Prussia, where the king himself had been one of the forerunners of the reform movement. It was only natural that Frederick II would be an admirer of Beccaria, and his feelings are shown clearly in a letter he wrote to Voltaire on September 5, 1777, saying: "Beccaria has left nothing to glean after him; we need only to follow what he has so wisely indicated." Frederick II had abolished torture soon after his accession to the throne, and in later years he decided to write a whole new criminal code. He died in 1786 before being able to finish his work, but the code was completed and put into effect by his successor. The new Prussian code was based largely on Beccaria's principles and although it did not abolish the death penalty, it nevertheless limited its application to very few cases.

In Russia, as we have already seen, Catherine II was not able to develop fully the great design she had had in mind originally; but she did take several progressive steps, one of them being the abolition of

---

16. For a survey of penal reforms in many lands before the end of the eighteenth century see Maestro, pp. 139–51.

torture. In Sweden law reforms were approved by the Act of Parliament of January 20, 1779.

In Tuscany the grand duke Leopold, the future Leopold II of Austria, decided in 1786 to promulgate a new code, based completely on Beccaria's principles: a just proportion between crimes and punishments, abolition of the penalties of confiscation and mutilation, abolition of torture and—a daring step—the complete abolition of the death penalty. In 1789 Leopold could already say: "We have experienced with the greatest satisfaction that mild laws together with a careful vigilance in the prevention of crimes, a speedy conclusion of the trial, promptness and certainty in the punishment applied to the real criminal, far from increasing the number of crimes, have considerably reduced the most common ones and have made the most atrocious almost disappear."[17]

In France the preparatory torture was abolished in 1780, but not until 1788, on the eve of the Revolution, were some more reforms announced, among them the abolition of the preliminary torture and the necessity of a majority of three votes instead of two in order to sustain a capital punishment. Even these limited changes remained on paper and it took the French Revolution to finally enact the great reforms. On October 9, 1789, a law of the Constituent Assembly approved the principles contained in the Declaration of the Rights of Man of August 26, 1789, among them the following, taken almost word for word from Beccaria's treatise: as to crimes, "the law has the right to prohibit only actions harmful to society"; as to penalties, "the law shall inflict only such punishments as are strictly and clearly necessary, and no one shall be punished, except in virtue of a law enacted before the offense and legally applied."

One of the most active members of the French assembly in the movement for penal reforms was General Lafayette who some years before had returned to France from America. Lafayette fought in the assembly for many democratic principles, such as popular representation, freedom of the press, suppression of privileged orders, religious tolerance, abolition of titles of nobility, and—in the field of criminal legislation—the establishment of trial by jury, an open and public procedure, the aid of counsel, and the abolition of arbitrary imprison-

---

17. The text of the Tuscan code of 1786 may be found in Beccaria, *Dei delitti e delle pene,* ed. Venturi, pp. 258–300; see also Cantù, pp. 250 ff.

ment. Lafayette's enlightened attitude was also shown by his opposition to the death penalty "as long as the infallibility of human judgment was not demonstrated." To his efforts must go the credit for the adoption by the assembly of many reforms in line with the new times. A law was also approved that abolished all punishments for so-called religious crimes; but we know, of course, that the revolutionary atmosphere was the cause of other excesses in the punishment of what were then considered political crimes. Moreover, as a reaction to previous customs the new laws went in many cases to reprehensible extremes in the opposite direction. But in later years, in a less emotional climate, new measures were taken which paved the way for a complete new set of laws, known as the Napoleonic Code, which went into effect on January 1, 1811. Despite several shortcomings, this new code represented a great step forward from the old cruelties and absurdities.[18]

In the Austrian empire Maria Theresa had been rather slow in accepting the new principles of Beccaria's treatise. Her code of 1769 had kept a theological basis and had retained torture, the pillory, branding, and corporal punishments—besides harsh penalties for blasphemy and apostasy from the Christian faith. Later, Maria Theresa became gradually more receptive to Beccaria's theories, and in 1776 torture was abolished under the influence of Sonnenfels. Much wider reforms were enacted by Maria Theresa's successor, Joseph II, who promulgated in 1787 a new penal code which, though still keeping in force the pillory and corporal punishments, adopted many of the new principles and, among other things, limited the death penalty to crimes of revolt against the state.

England, which had been the model of the eighteenth century, suddenly revealed the faults of its own system as soon as reforms had improved the laws of the continental countries. It is true that the English procedure had excellent features which were later accepted

---

18. For Lafayette's contribution to the penal reforms in the Constituent Assembly see *Mémoires, correspondance et manuscrits du général Lafayette, publiés par sa famille,* vol. 4, pp. 63 ff. (The complete name of General Lafayette was Marie Joseph Paul Yves Roch Gilbert du Motier, Marquis de La Fayette).

For Lafayette's attitude regarding the death penalty see Clark, *Crime in America—Observations on its Nature, Causes, Prevention and Control,* pp. 334–35. Clark's book, published in 1970, analyzes the vast problems of criminal justice in the United States in the twentieth century.

by other legislations, namely, the institution of the jury, the granting of a counsel to the accused person, and the rule that all trials be confrontative, oral, and public. But other aspects of the English legal system were less admirable and the reforms did not come readily. The *peine forte et dure* was abolished in 1772 and branding was eliminated in 1779. But other reforms were blocked by a strong group headed by Lord Ellenborough, a man of vast intellect and a legal scholar who believed that cruelty and terror were the only means of ensuring justice. Finally, in 1808, Romilly succeeded in repealing the statutes which punished by death small thefts committed without violence, and in 1816 the pillory was abolished in all cases except perjury. Other reforms had to wait much longer: in 1820 proposals to remove the capital penalty for such offenses as wounding cattle and destroying trees were accepted by the House of Commons, but did not pass the House of Lords. Only in 1832 was the punishment of death abolished for stealing a horse or a sheep, and the penalty of the pillory for perjury was not repealed until 1837.

In North America Beccaria was popular at a very early date, as shown by the words used by the future second president of the United States, John Adams, when as a young lawyer, in 1770, he took up the defense of the British soldiers implicated in what came to be called "The Boston Massacre." In front of an unfriendly court, in a crowded hall filled mostly with hostile and resentful people, John Adams rose to deliver his defense speech, and these were his opening words:

> May it please your honors, and you, gentlemen of the jury: I am for the prisoners at the bar, and shall apologize for it only in the words of the marquis Beccaria: If I can but be the instrument of preserving one life, his blessing and tears of transport shall be a sufficient consolation to me for the contempt of all mankind.[19]

John Adams's son, John Quincy Adams, wrote later that he often heard from spectators at the trial of the electrical effect produced by these words upon the jury and the "immense and excited auditory." John Adams spoke with eloquence and skill in defense of the British

---

19. For a complete coverage of the Boston trial see Kidder, *History of the Boston Massacre;* for John Adams's opening statement see p. 232. For the reaction of the public at Adams's first words see *The Works of John Adams,* vol. 2, pp. 238–39n.

soldiers and in the end none of them was found guilty of murder. All were set free immediately except two who were found guilty of manslaughter and were also discharged after being burnt on the hand. It was a great success for John Adams, who again mentioned Beccaria's words in his diary and added: "I have received such blessing, and enjoyed such tears of transport; and there is no greater pleasure and consolation."[20]

The great popularity of Beccaria in North America is shown also in the decisions taken some time later by the legislatures of the newly established states. It was Pennsylvania that led the way toward a more enlightened approach to the administration of justice. The attempt made earlier by William Penn to enact a humane and rational code of criminal laws for Pennsylvania had been thwarted by Queen Anne, but as soon as the state acquired its independence the revival of that code became an object of the first importance. In the writings of that period Beccaria is mentioned repeatedly as a primary influence on the renewed interest in penal reforms and on the laws that were soon enacted. Robert J. Turnbull discussed the penal laws in a series of articles which appeared in the *Charleston Daily Gazette* and were then edited and collected in his book *A Visit to the Philadelphia Prison*. This is what he wrote in one of his articles:

> Several circumstances combined to make the proposed alteration expedient, and among others the small and valuable gift of the immortal Beccaria to the world had its due influence and weight; for on the framing of the (then) new constitution of the state, in 1776, the legislature were directed *to proceed as soon as might be to the reformation of the penal laws and to invent punishments less sanguinary and better proportioned to the various degrees of criminality.*[21]

Because of the disruption caused by the war it took some time for these intentions to be carried out. Only in 1786 was the foundation of the desired reform laid by an act which reserved the punishment of death for four crimes: murder, rape, arson, and treason. At the same time the punishment of hard labor in public was introduced as

---

20. For the verdict and the conclusion of the Boston trial see Kidder, p. 285. For Adams's comment in his diary see *The Works of John Adams*, vol. 2, pp. 238–39.

21. The articles appeared in February 1796; see Turnbull, *A Visit to the Philadelphia Prison* (London), p. i; for our quotation and further passages concerning penal reforms in Pennsylvania see pp. 6 ff.

the penalty for many other major offenses. As explained by Turnbull, hard labor along the streets and roads gave negative results, since it toughened and embittered the criminals instead of reforming them. But in 1790 a new law abrogated public labor and in its place established private labor in penitentiaries. This experiment succeeded beyond all hopes. Finally, a further major step was taken when the Pennsylvania legislature approved a law that abolished the punishment of death for every crime except deliberate murder. This law, dated March 25, 1794, was called *An Act for the Better Preventing of Crimes and for Abolishing the Punishment of Death in Certain Cases* and it provided that "no crime whatsoever hereafter committed, except murder of the first degree, shall be punished with death in the state of Pennsylvania."[22]

The exemplary way in which the penitentiaries of Pennsylvania were run is described by Turnbull in an account which is indeed a classic report on a model institution. We will quote a few passages to illustrate what men can do when good sense and a compassionate spirit prevail.[23]

After calling the Philadelphia prison a "wonder of the world," Turnbull says: "The expression is comprehensive but no less just; for, of all the Bridewells or penitentiaries I ever read or heard of, I have met with none founded on similar principles, or which could in any manner boast of an administration so extensively useful and humane." Turnbull describes the various quarters of the prison and the workshops where men were busy on many activities, such as nail-manufacturing, marble-sawing and stone-cutting. In Turnbull's words: "There was such a spirit of industry visible on every side, and such contentment pervaded the countenances of all, that it was with difficulty I divested myself of the idea, that these men *surely were not* convicts, but accustomed to labour from their infancy."

Turnbull then describes the apartments of the women, where he saw them engaged in spinning cotton, carding wool, sewing, preparing flax and hemp, washing, and mending. Men and women, says Turnbull, are kept separate, and so are convicted criminals and untried prisoners; but no separation, he says, is kept between white

---

22. See *An Act for the Better Preventing of Crimes,* pp. 1 ff. (see bibliography under "Pennsylvania Statutes").
23. For his description of the Philadelphia prison see Turnbull, pp. 3 ff.

criminals and the negroes and mulattoes, who constitute about one-eighth of the number of convicts: "There are no degrading distinctions as in the Southern states, and at supper they all seat at the same table." We may note that these words were written in the eighteenth century by a man who had come from South Carolina. Turnbull says that he was also impressed by the cleanliness he found in every part of the Philadelphia prison and he points out another interesting fact: the prison, he learned, is self-supporting, since the work done by the inmates brings enough money to take care of all expenses and the state simply advances the needed funds and gets them back as soon as the proceeds from the workshop activities are collected.

The influence of Beccaria's ideas in Pennsylvania was so great that several prominent men went so far as to follow him in his stand for the complete abolition of the death penalty. In 1792 Dr. Benjamin Rush, a distinguished citizen and professor of clinical medicine at the University of Pennsylvania, published an essay entitled *Considerations of the Injustice and Impolicy of Punishing Murder by Death* in which he proclaimed that "the marquis of Beccaria has established a connexion between the abolition of capital punishment, and the order and happiness of society." To the objection that the Bible endorses the death penalty Dr. Rush answered that this is not so, and he analyzed biblical passages which, as interpreted by him, supported his point of view.[24]

Another writer who declared himself in favor of the complete abolition of the death penalty was the already mentioned Robert J. Turnbull. He discussed the problem with deep insight, using many arguments left untouched by Dr. Rush, among them the favorable results obtained in places where the death penalty had been abolished. Turnbull recalls that the grand duke of Tuscany, Leopold, "soon after the publication of the marquis of Beccaria's excellent treatise on this subject abolished death as a punishment for murder." After Leopold's decision, Turnbull points out, very few murders were com-

---

24. See Rush, *Considerations of the Injustice and Impolicy of Punishing Murder by Death,* pp. 3 ff. Dr. Benjamin Rush (1745–1813) studied medicine at Edinburgh and became one of the first American physicians to achieve an international reputation. Active also in political and social life, in 1774 he founded with James Pemberton an antislavery society and in 1776, as a member of Congress from Pennsylvania, he was a signer of the Declaration of Independence.

mitted in Tuscany, proportionately fewer than in the Italian states where the death penalty was maintained. Turnbull endorses Beccaria's legal and moral reasons for the abolition of capital punishment and he concludes his plea with the words: "The punishment of death thus ascertained to be an encroachment on the rights of the citizen, I would wish to go one step further than the legislature of Pennsylvania—I should be happy to observe it abolished even in the case of murder."[25]

The laws enacted in Pennsylvania and the enlightened views expressed by many citizens of that state were studied with great interest in the neighboring state of Virginia. We find another proof of Beccaria's early popularity on the American continent in Thomas Jefferson's *Commonplace Book* which contains several extracts from Montesquieu in French, followed by no less than twenty-six extracts from Beccaria in Italian, all long passages cited in Jefferson's own handwriting. These extracts were written, according to Gilbert Chinard who edited the *Commonplace Book,* between 1774 and 1776, when Jefferson became a member of the Virginia Committee of Revisors for the reform of the legal system. Criminal law was Jefferson's field and at the end of 1778 he had already completed his "Bill for Proportioning Crimes and Punishments in Cases heretofore Capital." This bill is copiously annotated, and Beccaria's name appears four times in footnotes which refer to several passages of his famous treatise. Not until 1785 was the bill introduced in the House of the Virginia Commonwealth; it was rejected then, but it was later approved when presented again in 1796. In his autobiography Jefferson describes these events as follows:

> Beccaria, and other writers on crimes and punishments, had satisfied the reasonable world of the unrightfulness and inefficacy of the punishment of crimes by death; and hard labor on roads, canals and other public works, had been suggested as a proper substitute. The Revisors had adopted these opinions; but the general idea of our country had not yet advanced to that point. The bill, therefore, for proportioning crimes and punishments was lost in the House of Delegates by a majority of a single vote. . . . In the meanwhile, the public opinion was ripening, by time, by reflection, and by the example of

---

25. See Turnbull, pp. 49 ff.

Pennsylvania. . . . In 1796 our legislature resumed the subject, and passed the law for amending the penal laws of the Commonwealth.[26]

This law followed closely Beccaria's principles and limited the death penalty to crimes of treason and murder.

It is interesting to note that Jefferson agreed with Beccaria on the advisability of not granting pardons in a system of mild laws. Referring to two types of pardons mentioned in an article that had come to his attention, Jefferson commented: "When laws are made as mild as they should be, both these pardons are absurd. The principle of Beccaria is sound. Let the legislators be merciful, but the executors of the law inexorable."[27]

As pointed out by Jefferson in his autobiography, the attitude of the people in Virginia had been influenced by the laws that had been enacted in Pennsylvania, notably the law that had abolished the death penalty except in case of wilful murder. At the same time Jefferson noted that in Pennsylvania the experiment of hard labor on the highways had not been successful because the criminals, exhibited as a public spectacle, had been driven into desperation and further depravity. We have seen, however, that in Pennsylvania the system of hard labor in secluded penitentiaries had worked well, and this system was soon imitated in Virginia and elsewhere. As regards the death penalty, it became an object of debate in several states and another important step was taken when the legislature of Ohio approved a law limiting capital punishment in that state to deliberate murder. We may say with confidence that we owe it in great measure to Beccaria if laws were enacted which reduced considerably the number of executions in the newly established American states.

The first laws of the federal government also show the influence of the new ideas, as well as that of the English procedure. In 1787 the

---

26. See *The Commonplace Book of Thomas Jefferson, A Repertory of his Ideas on Government*, ed. Chinard. The dates of the transcriptions from Beccaria are given by Chinard in the introduction, pp. 38–39. The transcriptions are on pp. 298–316.

For the quotations from Jefferson's autobiography see *The Writings of Thomas Jefferson*, vol. 1, pp. 67 ff. For the text of the "Bill for Proportioning Crimes and Punishments in Cases heretofore Capital" see *The Writings of Thomas Jefferson*, vol. 1, pp. 218 ff.

27. This observation was made by Jefferson in a comment to an article entitled "Etats Unis," prepared for the *Encyclopédie Méthodique*. See *The Complete Jefferson*, ed. Padover, p. 61.

Constitution of the United States provided that "the trial of all crimes, except in cases of impeachment, shall be by jury." Other provisions were added in the amendments to the Constitution which were adopted some years later. They specified that the accused was entitled to a speedy and public trial, and that he had the right to be confronted with witnesses against him, to obtain witnesses in his favor and to have the assistance of counsel for his defense. Moreover: "Excessive bail shall not be required, nor excessive fines imposed, nor cruel and unusual punishments inflicted." Finally, provisions were made to keep the legislative and executive powers separate and distinct from the judiciary, not only in the federal government, but in all the American states. While the influence of the English tradition is visible in many of these measures, there is no doubt that the writings of Beccaria and of the other reformers were responsible for the attitude that prevailed in a number of resolutions adopted in the new nation.[28]

One place has not been mentioned in this review of penal reforms: the very place from which had come the famous book that had inspired this whole movement, the province of Lombardy. Ironically, in the land of Beccaria only minor changes had taken place in the years that followed the publication of his treatise, and when, in 1787, the emperor Joseph II promulgated the new Austrian code, it was decided not to extend it to Lombardy where conditions were not the same as in the dominions of Central Europe. But in 1791, as we have seen, a special commission was appointed in Milan, by order of the new emperor Leopold II, to study the possibility of extending the code to Lombardy with those changes that might be found advisable for a province of different character and traditions; and Beccaria had been designated by the emperor himself to be a member of that commission.

---

28. For more information on laws and provisions adopted in the federal and state constitutions of the United States see Poore, *The Federal and State Constitutions, Colonial Charters and Other Organic Laws of the United States.* vol. 1, pp. 18 ff.

11

The Commission for
the New Lombard Code

As a member of the economic council, Beccaria had had the opportunity of giving practical effect to many of his ideas in the economic field. Similarly, as a member of the commission for the new Lombard code, he would now be able to participate in the legal reforms that he had advocated in his youthful treatise. It took some time, however, for the commission to be organized, and in the meantime Beccaria was asked by the government to give his personal view on the Austrian code, which had been suggested as a model for the future code of Lombardy. Beccaria presented his comments in a report in which he touched on some articles of the code that seemed to him open to criticism.[1]

In his report, dated simply 1791, Beccaria makes a distinction between major crimes and minor crimes (the latter were called in Italian, improperly, *delitti politici*) and he tries to define the two. He says that by major crimes he means crimes tending to the destruc-

---

1. For the full text of Beccaria's report containing his personal comments on the Austrian code see Beccaria, *Opere,* ed. Romagnoli, vol. 2, pp. 705–18. The report is entitled "Brevi riflessioni intorno al codice generale sopra i delitti e le pene, per ciò che riguarda i delitti politici."

tion of the social bond; by minor crimes he means transgressions which, although damaging society, do not tend to destroy it. This difference, explains Beccaria, implies different types of penalties: the main goal of punishments for major crimes should be to deter others from committing similar offenses, while the first purpose of penalties for minor crimes should be the correction of the individual. Therefore, while reaffirming his opposition to the death penalty, Beccaria asserts that those guilty of major crimes should receive long and harsh punishments that have a deterrent effect on other potential criminals, while minor crimes should be met with smaller penalties aimed in the first place at correcting the wrongdoer.

Having made this distinction, Beccaria notes that the Austrian code provides instead the same type of penalty for major and minor crimes, the difference between the two being only the duration or intensity of the penalty. Thus the pillory and flogging are prescribed for minor as well as major crimes; but these are penalties, says Beccaria, which bring infamy and disgrace to the convicted man, and instead of correcting him they are likely to push him to greater crimes. Beccaria is especially concerned about people of noble or distinguished families. He does not object to the same penalties being administered to all people convicted of major crimes, but he is convinced that a person of high standing would suffer more than an illiterate laborer when subjected to the same infamous penalty, and he feels this factor should be taken into consideration in the case of a minor crime. This is not a departure from the principle of an equal law for all, says Beccaria; on the contrary, the distinction of classes in the case of minor crimes is necessary in order to bring about the desired equality. Always considering that the correction of the individual is the aim of punishment for a minor crime, Beccaria explains: "Flogging may perhaps correct an ignorant fellow of humble condition, but it certainly would dishearten and ruin a gentleman, an honest merchant, a well-bred person; and his whole family would feel covered with the most horrible shame. Then the punishment is no longer proportionate to the crime, it is incomparably greater."

This idea, that different penalties for different kinds of people bring about a greater equality, is new in Beccaria's thought. This concept had not appeared in his treatise where, on the contrary, he had stated that the same punishment should be inflicted on every culprit, noble or plebeian, because the measure of punishments cannot be the sensibility of the criminal, but the public injury. Beccaria seems also to contradict here his principle that the law must be clearly written and that the judge's job is to apply it to anyone who is found guilty. Now it appears that Beccaria would give a judge some leeway on the basis of the guilty person's position in society, and all this to avoid inflicting greater suffering on a person of higher rank than on a humble citizen.

There is at least a partial explanation for this change in Beccaria's attitude, which may seem at first a withdrawal from the high moral principles upheld in his early treatise. The fact is that Beccaria had little sympathy for the so-called infamous penalties which had been preserved in the Austrian code. Faced by the possibility of having these penalties extended to Lombardy even for minor crimes, he says that at least the people of a certain rank should be spared being disgraced by them. In his treatise Beccaria could afford to be adamant about certain principles; but now he was dealing with practical measures, and some compromise, perhaps not praiseworthy, seemed to him necessary. That Beccaria was in general against this kind of penalty is shown by the following remarks:

> The Milanese people are docile, obedient, not prone to violence; they need encouragement and a better education more than the fear of harsh punishments for minor crimes. . . . Imprisonment should be the regular penalty for minor crimes, a more or less long term according to the offense. . . . Prisons for minor crimes should be separate from those housing major criminals; and the possibility of house confinement should be studied for small infractions.

In his observations on minor crimes Beccaria then agrees with the Austrian code that even some of the more serious crimes, like robberies, frauds, and public scandals should be treated as minor crimes when they are committed for the first time: "A first act, wicked as it may be, does not necessarily mean habitual malice and does not preclude the possibility that the guilty individual may be corrected." However, the same crime committed a second time, says Beccaria, puts the wrongdoer in the category of a major criminal. In fact, adds Beccaria, the Austrian code does not seem severe enough toward those who have repeatedly committed the same offense.

Two more points are dealt with by Beccaria in his personal comments on the Austrian code. The first concerns adultery, which in the

Austrian code was considered a minor crime. Beccaria accepts this definition, but says that the importance of the marriage bond, which is a sort of mutual property and is the basis of the family, of the children's education, of social relations, and inheritance rights, may well make adultery, since it undermines the marriage bond, a major crime. However, accepting adultery as a minor crime, Beccaria would like to make some distinction between the man and the woman. An adulteress, he says, may give to her husband children who are not his, while a man who commits adultery with a loose woman does not harm society to the same extent; consequently, he deserves a lesser punishment than an adulteress. Of course, Beccaria's attitude in this respect is questionable because a man who commits adultery may give a woman children who would grow up without a father. Wouldn't this act harm society as much as that of an adulterous wife? We must add, however, that Beccaria's theory is presented in general terms and does not exclude a different approach for specific cases. At any rate, Beccaria agrees with the Austrian code in its provision that punishment for adultery should be inflicted only upon the request of the injured party and only when this party is innocent of similar dealings.

The last point on which Beccaria gives his views is prostitution. The Austrian code had prohibited the exercise of prostitution and had prescribed penalties for those guilty of it. Beccaria is against this prohibition: it is an evil, he says, which in large cities seems unavoidable if we don't want to push the young men toward attempts at much more harmful relations with honest ladies and married women. "It seems right to punish prostitution when it is accompanied by scandalous and open seduction," concludes Beccaria, "but otherwise it seems wise to treat it as a necessary evil and let it go at that."

Besides presenting to the government his personal comments on some aspects of the Austrian code, Beccaria also made suggestions concerning improvements in the conditions of inmates in the penitentiaries and prisons of Lombardy. In the meantime the commission for the new Lombard code had begun its work, and Beccaria took an active part in it. The commission, whose task was to submit concrete proposals for the new code, was composed of seven members, some of whom had been appointed on Beccaria's suggestion; but its work had a slow start and a year later several points were still under discussion, among them the question of the death penalty, on which the various members held divergent views. The Tuscan code had abol-

ished capital punishment, and the Austrian code to all practical purposes had done the same, since it had retained the death penalty only
for cases of revolt against the state. These were the two codes that
the commission had been invited to study and to follow whenever
possible in the preparation of the new Lombard code. But Beccaria
had a hard time trying to convince all the other members to follow
the example of the two model codes in regard to the death penalty.
When, in 1792, it became clear that the two attitudes within the commission could not be reconciled, it was decided to prepare separate
reports and to continue the debate at a later date.

The report proposing the abolition of the death penalty was signed
by Beccaria and by two other members, Gallarati-Scotti and Risi. It
repeated in part what Beccaria had written in his treatise *On Crimes
and Punishments;* but since this report was limited to purely legal
arguments, the appeal to humanity contained in the treatise was
absent here. On the other hand, we find in the report some new
points against the death penalty: first, the experience of those countries, such as Tuscany, where the death penalty had been abolished
and where the crime rate had diminished; and second, a point that
Beccaria had omitted in his treatise, the irrevocability and finality of
the death penalty. The report recalled cases in which errors were
made which could not be repaired. Absolute proofs sufficient for
sentencing a man to death simply do not exist, said the report; even
the testimony of more than one witness, even the confession of the
accused man, do not give us this certainty, as shown by actual cases
in which these supposedly certain proofs turned out to be false after
the accused had been executed.

As in Beccaria's treatise, the report admitted one theoretical case
in which the death penalty would be admissible: the case of an
apprehended man who, although strictly guarded, was still in a position to subvert the state through external connections. This would be
like an act of war, not foreseeable in a peaceful society.

The report then contained a general appeal for a system of inexorable but moderate laws which would in turn make men more
moderate. It also suggested that the punishments replacing the death
penalty be in full view: the penitentiaries should be established, not
in remote places, but near the cities as a useful example of the consequence of crimes to as many people as possible, an example that
would have a deterring influence on those who might be tempted to
commit criminal acts. The death penalty, the report finally warned,

may be the quickest way to get rid of a culprit, but not the most effective way to suppress crime.

The other members of the commission for the new code had different opinions and made them known in separate reports in which they declared themselves in favor of the death penalty for criminals convicted of deliberate murder. The advocates of the death penalty contended that, contrary to Beccaria's unproved statement, the death penalty is more of a preventive of crime than confinement for life: nothing, they said, scares a potential criminal more than the risk of being executed. Besides, they added, who can be sure that a convicted criminal may never escape from a penitentiary and endanger again the life of innocent people? If the death penalty in Lombardy is abolished, they also said, there is the additional risk that criminals will be attracted here from other countries where the death penalty exists. As regards the irrevocability of the death penalty, the defenders of capital punishment maintained that this penalty should be inflicted only if absolute certainty of guilt existed. They said at this point: "If we accept the theory that there cannot be absolute certainty in the proofs of guilt in a trial, then we must deny the possibility of human certainty in anything—indeed we should put in doubt everything we know." In the end the defenders of the death penalty expressed their confidence that the refusal to abolish capital punishment would contribute to saving, if not the property, at least the life of many honest citizens.[2]

The cold reasoning of Beccaria's adversaries in the commission for the new code undoubtedly had some legal merit and showed that Beccaria's theories about the death penalty were not foolproof. It is true that he had now added the idea of the irrevocability of the death penalty, but his adversaries showed that not even that argument was a decisive one. Perhaps the most important point in favor of the abolition was Beccaria's theory that a system of inexorable but moderate laws would contribute to molding the character of the people accordingly, making them kinder and gentler, less prone to commit crimes. Even this theory, although supported by the experience of several nations, was not necessarily valid in every situation and under all circumstances.

---

2. For the text of the report favoring the abolition of the death penalty see Beccaria, *Opere,* ed. Romagnoli, vol. 2, pp. 735–41; or Cantù, pp. 369–74. For the reports presented by other members of the commission who opposed the abolition of the death penalty see Cantù, pp. 357 ff.

In the end it is perhaps only a question of personal feeling: whether or not human life should be considered sacred. Beccaria felt that it should. For him any killing, including the execution of a criminal, was an evil act; he simply could not accept the fact that the head of a man might be tendered to another man, hired to cut it. Beccaria's abhorrence of violence and bloodshed extended to war itself, although in his treatise he had seemed helpless in the face of it; there he had spoken of war as a "necessity," adding that in any case the laws should not extend that "savage example" by committing public murders.

As a matter of fact, it is hard to decide which type of killing is more savage and it may be of interest to recall that not many years after Beccaria a French writer, Joseph de Maistre, described the killing in war as much more repulsive and barbarous than the killing of a criminal. In a book entitled *Soirées de Saint Pétersbourg* de Maistre, who was no enemy of the death penalty, wrote a panegyric on the executioner. He imagines in his story that someone from space comes to talk to some people on earth, and the conversation turns to the subject of killing. The inhabitants of our planet tell their visitor that two kinds of men have the authorization from the public power to kill other men. One of these kills criminals after they have been convicted of terrible deeds; such executions are so rare, however, that one of these men is sufficient for a whole province. The other kills as many men as he can, and he generally kills honest people. One of these two professional killers is greatly honored; the other is looked upon with great contempt. Of course, the visitor from space, not knowing anything about military glory, guesses wrong about who is honored and who is despised.[3]

Joseph de Maistre's preference for the executioner is not shared by the majority of people, perhaps because soldiers risk their own lives or because they seem often to be the helpless tools of more powerful persons. At any rate, it was Beccaria's conviction that violent crimes are bound to be committed in a society in which men are authorized or directed by their government to kill other people, and for him the abolition of the death penalty was a necessary step toward that gentler civilization to which he aspired.

---

3. For this excerpt from Joseph de Maistre's *Soirées de Saint Pétersbourg* and comments by Cantù see Cantù, pp. 282–83.

12

The Final Years

THE commission for the new Lombard code continued its debates in several sessions, but the discussions were fruitless and no practical results were reached. At any rate, by then the political events in Europe made everything seem temporary and precarious.

Beccaria's private life was beset by more troubles. The marriage of his daughter Giulia and Pietro Manzoni became increasingly difficult, and in 1791 she asked Pietro Verri to intervene with her father and help her obtain a separation. She told Verri that life with her husband had become impossible and that her father, who had pushed her into this marriage, did not understand the situation. Beccaria, however, turned out to be less stubborn than she thought, and he made the arrangement for a separation that from a financial point of view was quite favorable to his daughter. Giulia, who was only thirty, then became very fond of a gentleman by the name of Imbonati and lived with him, in London and Paris, until he died in 1805. Later on she lived in Italy, a very wealthy lady who had inherited by then her share of her father's property and also some money from her friend Imbonati as well as from her husband Manzoni. We may add that, after she had overcome the feeling of bitterness caused by her unhappy marriage, she showed constant pride in her father's accomplishments.

Beccaria's son, Giulio, who was seventeen years old in 1792, always remained close to him. He was a serious young man who had a boundless admiration for his father. In later years and during his whole life he treasured his father's memory, and it is to his patience and devotion that we owe the preservation of Beccaria's letters, papers, and scattered notes.

In 1792 Beccaria was fifty-four and his health was not good. He was overweight and he still liked to eat well even though he should have been more careful. Perhaps feeling the danger of a sudden collapse, he decided to guarantee, in case of his death, an annuity of 12,000 lire for his wife. Of course, this grant cut into his assets, and his two brothers promptly started legal proceedings against him in an attempt to have this provision annulled. Apparently they were not successful in their effort, but by their behavior they certainly made Beccaria's life more miserable. It is ironic that this man, who in his whole life never initiated legal actions against anyone, was in constant legal trouble, sued at every turn by one or another of his relatives.

The last two years of Beccaria's life were not happy ones and his only comfort was his little family: his wife and young Giulio. In his office he continued to write his reports and to submit proposals on various matters. His last paper, dated April 3, 1794, was a study of the sanitary situation in Lombardy, with suggestions on how to better organize that department. But all seemed unimportant now that the French Revolution had become a bloody spectacle threatening to engulf the neighboring countries.

It had all started promisingly with the Declaration of the Rights of Man, in which several of Beccaria's principles had been incorporated. The declaration was approved by a law that the Constituent Assembly enacted in October of 1789, and at the insistence of General Lafayette several other liberal laws were adopted by the assembly in the following months. Then, on May 30, 1791, a debate took place on the death penalty. The first speaker was a deputy from Nancy, Jacques-Pierre Prugnon, who asked that capital punishment be maintained for those guilty of murder. We want to know, he said, if man has handed over to society the right to dispose of his life: the great Beccaria affirms that he has not, but many others have expressed a different view. And here Prugnon mentioned Montesquieu, Rousseau, and Filangieri among those who had upheld the death penalty. In the case of murder, asserted Prugnon, there should be no doubt: he who puts an end to the existence of a fellowman should pay for his crime with his own life.[1]

In that memorable session, a young lawyer then came to the rostrum: he was Maximilien Robespierre, a deputy from Arras, where he had been appointed criminal judge but had then resigned as he did not want to pronounce a death sentence. Robespierre spoke for an hour with great eloquence, stressing all of Beccaria's reasons for the abolition of capital punishment and ending his oration with the following words:

> The laws must be models of justice and reason, not examples of anger and revenge; above all, they have no right to order that a man's blood be shed. . . . Human life must be sacred, and when the public power plays with it, then the dignity of man is diminished; and the idea of murder ceases to terrify us if the law itself gives us an example of it. We should not think that crimes are discouraged by cruel laws and excessive punishments. The opposite is true: it is in the free and civilized countries, where laws are just and mild, that crimes are rare. Instead, where the laws offend humanity with their excessive harshness, there the dignity of man is ignored and there the legislator is a master who rules over slaves and punishes them without pity. For all these reasons I propose that the death penalty be abrogated.[2]

The members of the assembly listened intently to Robespierre's ardent plea, but the majority did not agree with him and three days later a law was approved that upheld the preservation of the death penalty and specified that in the future "all executions shall be carried out by decapitation." Until then an axe had been used for the gruesome task, but in 1792 a beheading machine was perfected by a physician, Dr. Guillotin, and adopted in France for all executions.

---

1. For the account of the session held in Paris on May 30, 1791, by the French Constituent Assembly see Firpo, *"Dei delitti e delle pene" di Cesare Beccaria, facsimile dell'edizione originale,* pp. 183 ff. For more details on the sessions of the Constituent Assembly and the laws passed in 1789 and following years see Bar, *A History of Continental Criminal Law,* pp. 320 ff.; also Esmein, *Histoire de la procédure criminelle en France,* pp. 410–50.

2. The full text of Robespierre's speech in the assembly of May 30, 1791, was published in the *Gazette nationale, ou le Moniteur universel,* Paris, no. 162, June 1, 1791, pp. 630–31, as indicated in Firpo, p. 190. An Italian translation of Robespierre's speech may be found in Firpo, pp. 184–90.

Soon there were not enough of these machines for the many heads that had to fall. Louis XVI was executed in January of 1793 and the queen, Marie Antoinette, followed his fate a few months later. Lafayette, who had tried in vain to moderate the excesses of the Revolution, was declared a traitor by the assembly and had to flee the country in order to save his life. Once in Belgium he was held prisoner first by the Prussians and then by the Austrians, who accused him of having been one of the promoters of the Revolution.[3]

A Committee of Public Safety now ruled Paris without any regard for justice or human life. Among the members of the committee three men acquired prominence: St. Just, Couthon, and more than any other, Robespierre. The man who not so long before had spoken against the death penalty was now the soul of the Terror, sending to the guillotine hundreds of his own former friends and followers in a fanatical pursuit of twisted ideals. The guillotine finally caught up with him, when the Convention ordered his arrest and execution on July 28, 1794.

From Milan Beccaria had followed with a heavy heart the terrible course of events. He had advocated fairness in the administration of justice, and the courts of justice of the nation he had admired so much had now become courts of condemnation without trial. He had advocated the abolition of the death penalty even for the worst crimes as a necessary step toward a more civilized society, and thousands of citizens were being beheaded, often without a conviction, in an immense sacrifice to the bloodthirsty men in power.

Did Beccaria understand that the Reign of Terror was a dreadful but passing stage of the French Revolution? Did he foresee that after these extreme and absurd reactions a new society would go back to those reforms that he had advocated and that, in fact, had already been accepted in many countries? We do not know what Beccaria thought at the end of his life. Perhaps he was able to keep some hope for a more distant future, but in the meantime the world around him seemed to be crumbling, that orderly world of the Austrian empire and of his Lombardy that he had worked hard to improve in so many ways. Also the threat of war was becoming more and more real.

---

3. Lafayette was finally released from prison thanks to a stipulation made by Napoleon in the treaty of Campo-Formio (October 1797). He returned to France in 1799 after having been held prisoner for five years.

Saddened by what was happening, fearful of worse things to come, he had the presentiment that his end was near and he was afraid of being left alone. One day, however—November 28, 1794—he was alone in the house and later was found dead of apoplexy. Perhaps a prompt intervention might have prolonged his life; he was not yet fifty-seven years old.

With a very simple funeral and without any special ceremony he was buried in the cemetery of San Gregorio. No one except his wife and son seemed to care about Beccaria's passing. In the turmoil of a rapidly changing world his death went almost unnoticed even in his native city. There was no word of it in the newspapers, nor were speeches made to honor or praise him. This silence may well appear as a last tribute to his modesty and to his feeling of uneasiness at being in the limelight. Some time later, at the grave in which he was buried his son Giulio laid a simple stone with a Latin inscription saying that there lay Cesare Beccaria, "councillor in the public administration, expert in criminal jurisprudence, writer of clear intellect."[4]

If someone had spoken a few words when the stone was laid, he might have said what Cesare Cantù wrote many years later in his study of Beccaria. Cantù spoke of Beccaria the human being, of his character and feelings:

> They say that Beccaria was a timid man. What does that matter if as a writer he showed great courage? He was without malice or rancor, he never felt envy or jealousy toward other members of his profession, as is so often the case in the literary world. His serenity and his gentleness never failed when he was faced by domestic troubles or by the haughty indifference of those who tried to deprive him of his self-confidence. His wisdom enabled him to ignore the arrows of malevolence, and he became closed in himself and adopted an attitude of reserve in order not to feel hate or enmity toward anyone. He always loved a simple life and seemed embarrassed by applause and public honor. He had praises for the rulers, having no revolutionary instinct or aspiration, but he criticized what he considered wrong or harmful in their rule. He thought that it was noble to respect the laws, but also that it was his duty to examine them and to expose their faults with frankness and dignity; and whatever his dependent position, his mind and his soul remained always free.[5]

---

4. For the Latin words of the epitaph on Beccaria's tomb see Cantù, p. 173.
5. See Cantù, pp. 154–60. Ours is a free and condensed version of Cantù's appraisal.

This is how Cantù in his book described Beccaria, and it was, we think, a fair appraisal.

It did not take long for the French Revolution to spread to other countries. At the beginning of 1796 the young new general of the French army, Napoleon Bonaparte, led his soldiers across the Alps, telling them that they were heading toward "the rich provinces of northern Italy." After a series of victories over the Piedmontese and Austrian armies the French entered Milan in May of 1796 under the banner of liberty, equality and fraternity. With one of their first decrees they proclaimed the abolition of all titles of nobility, and the former Count Pietro Verri wrote to his brother in Rome: "From now on please address your letters simply: Citizen Pietro Verri. I never liked titles anyway and if I used mine it was only because others did. . . . I don't now feel deprived of anything, only an empty illusion has disappeared."[6]

Almost seventy years old, Verri had lost many illusions and saw now in a clearer perspective the results of his life work, of his struggles and ambitions. Since he was one of the prominent men in Milan, the French authorities asked him to be a member of the municipal council, which was to act temporarily as a city government under French control. Verri accepted the office rather reluctantly because his hearing was now weak. He showed little enthusiasm for the new activity and he rarely spoke in the council; but at a session held a few weeks before the end of 1796 Citizen Verri rose to remind his colleagues that Cesare Beccaria had been dead for more than two years. It was a speech that he addressed to the council, but perhaps also to himself: "Where is the monument to Beccaria," he asked, "the monument that you Milanese have erected to that immortal genius who first proclaimed that the goal of social science must be the greatest happiness shared by the greatest number? How have you shown your gratitude to the man who gave luster to your city, whose book on justice has been translated in all languages and is now placed among the most sublime works in all the world libraries?. . . . It would be unforgivable not to honor now the great man who dared,

---

6. See Casati, vol. 4, pp. 211–12, Pietro Verri's letter to Alessandro of May 28, 1796.

not without danger, to defend the cause of the oppressed and who opened the way to the triumph of justice and humanity."[7]

This was Pietro Verri's last speech; he died very soon after. His brother Alessandro also had second thoughts about Beccaria. In a letter written some years later, in 1803, Alessandro recalled how the treatise *On Crimes and Punishments* had been written by Beccaria in the room of the Accademia dei Pugni and how Pietro had made a fair copy of it from Beccaria's script, which was full of erasures and corrections. "Pietro was foreseeing for Beccaria the applause of all Europe," wrote Alessandro, "and I had the same conviction."[8]

This interesting confession was made nine years after Beccaria's death. Despite Pietro's speech, no monuments to Beccaria were then built in Milan. There were too many other problems to be solved in those years, and three decades were to pass before a monument to Beccaria was finally erected by the Milanese. In later years schools, streets, and squares were named after him all over Italy, a country finally independent and no longer divided. His most successful book, the treatise *On Crimes and Punishments,* was printed again and again in many languages. His other accomplishments were increasingly appreciated and his farsightedness in many fields was recognized. Several Italian editions of all his writings were published and the most important encyclopedias of all countries spoke of him.[9]

In 1964, two hundred years after the publication of *On Crimes and Punishments,* the event was commemorated with special meetings in several European cities: Rome, Milan, Turin, and Frankfurt. The celebrations of Rome and Milan were sponsored by the Italian Lincei Academy in cooperation with the United Nations Economic and Social Council, those of Turin were sponsored by the Science Acad-

---

7. See Cantù, p. 248, and Beccaria, *Opere,* ed. Romagnoli, vol. 1, pp. xcvii–xcviii. For the full text of the speech, which dealt also with other subjects, see Pietro Verri, *Scritti vari,* vol. 2, Appendice, pp. 89 ff.

8. See Vianello, pp. 72–74.

9. The impression has been given by some superficial critics that the publication of the treatise *On Crimes and Punishments* marked the end of Beccaria's creative activity, but all serious scholars of Beccaria—among them Cantù, Mondolfo, Romagnoli, and Venturi—fully recognized the importance of his other works. Vianello is a special case: he was enough interested in Beccaria to do patient research on his activity in the economic council of Milan and to edit for the first time some of his writings, but often there is sourness and lack of sympathy in his comments.

emy of Turin, and the meeting in Frankfurt was organized by the German Criminological Society. Jurists and scholars from many countries participated in the ceremonies and all stressed Beccaria's enduring greatness. Speeches were made in many languages, but little was said in English because—this is indeed difficult to explain—few representatives came from England or the United States, two countries where Beccaria had been most popular and influential.[10]

Although many of Beccaria's works are worthy of attention and study, his fame is based primarily on his treatise *On Crimes and Punishments* and it is easy to understand the reason for its success. All the jurists before Beccaria, even the most famous ones, had been cold and impersonal. He showed, instead, that in the conduct of human affairs the guidance of reason, although necessary, may become tyrannical and absurd if not supplemented by the human feelings which come from the heart. While others had analyzed every facet and angle of all legal problems without seeing their human basis, Beccaria went directly to their essence and said in simple terms some very important things.

Beccaria put the problem of punishments on a new plane, stating that the purpose of penalties is not retribution, but prevention: justice requires a right proportion between crimes and punishments, but the purpose of penalties is to prevent a criminal from doing more harm and to deter others from doing similar damage. Beccaria was convinced that man remains barbaric if he inflicts cruel punishments, that he degrades himself by becoming a spy, that he becomes accustomed to bloodshed if he is exposed to it. Beccaria wanted a society of kind and civilized people and he believed that the abolition of cruel punishments, including the death penalty, would contribute to

---

10. Of the many papers presented during the celebrations held in 1964 in honor of Beccaria only two were written in the English language: "Beccaria and Bentham" by H.L.A. Hart, and "Cesare Beccaria and the English System of Criminal Justice: A Reciprocal Relationship" by Leon Radzinowicz. Both papers were presented at the meeting organized by the Turin Academy.

For details on the above celebrations and the text of speeches and lectures see *Accademia Nazionale dei Lincei, Problemi attuali di scienza e cultura, Quaderno no. 71* (for the meetings in Rome and Milan), *Accademia delle Scienze di Torino, Atti del Convegno internazionale su Cesare Beccaria, Memorie— Classe di scienze morali, serie IV, no. 9* (for the meeting in Turin), and *Deutsche Kriminologische Gesellschaft, Cesare Beccaria "Dei delitti e delle pene," Zweihundert Jahre später, 1764–1964* (for the meeting in Frankfurt). See bibliography for complete data.

the formation of such a society. In this sense his approach was moral rather than juridical, so that Beccaria may be considered not so much a leading criminologist as a builder of a more civilized society and of a better and more pleasant world. His principles in many fields were subordinate to one higher aspiration: the moral progress of mankind. In his essay on style he had written: "Morality, politics, and the fine arts all have their origin in one first science, the science of man." This ability to see everything in human terms makes Beccaria stand out above the other jurists and above the specialists, and it explains why he was able to inspire so many people and lead the nations of the world on the paths he advocated.

Beccaria had had the satisfaction of seeing in his lifetime the first results of his efforts when penal reforms were enacted in many countries, and we must hope that he was not too disheartened by the excesses of the French Revolution. We know that the Revolution was, in fact, the outcome of the philosophical movement of the eighteenth century, and once the extreme reactions had died down and peace in Europe was reestablished, the reform movement was resumed and a new society put into practice most of the principles for which so many enlightened men had ardently fought.

Yet no conquest is ever definitive and this is the reason for Beccaria's perennial actuality. In his treatise *On Crimes and Punishments* he had said: "The happy time has not yet arrived in which truth shall be the possession of the greater number, as error has been so far." This statement is still valid today and the better world for which Beccaria strove is not yet here. Far from it: we have seen in this twentieth century a return to some of the worst and most cruel practices of past ages, and instead of the world without bloodshed of which Beccaria dreamt we have witnessed new wars fought with the most terrible and destructive weapons and the murder of millions of innocent people.

Today it is not easy to look at the future of mankind with confidence. Everywhere new problems have arisen, brought about by an unchecked and at times perhaps purposeless technological advance and by an ever-growing population for which the future appears bleak and uncertain. We like to say that the world has become smaller, and in a sense it has; but it has also become more complex, since it is no longer divided into tight compartments, and what happens today on one continent is immediately felt everywhere else. The

European reformers of the eighteenth century never thought of any part of the world outside Europe and the territories settled by Europeans. Today the horizon is wider, and different ideas and traditions confront each other. However, the basic principles of human conduct are the same everywhere because all people on earth are moved by the same fundamental drives and impulses. Beccaria's dream of a peaceful society in which truth and justice will prevail is still a dream; but he did make his contribution to a more hopeful future, and his spirit still inspires those who do not want to be discouraged and who strive and work for a better world.

BIBLIOGRAPHY

Accademia delle Scienze di Torino: Atti del Convegno internazionale su Cesare Beccaria promosso dall'Accademia delle Scienze di Torino nel secondo centenario dell'opera "Dei delitti e delle pene." Turin: Memorie dell'Accademia delle Scienze, Classe di scienze morali, serie IV, no. 9, 1966.

Accademia Nazionale dei Lincei — Problemi attuali di scienza e cultura, Quaderno no. 71 (containing records of celebrations in honor of Beccaria sponsored by the Lincei Academy and UNESCO in Rome and Milan, June 1964). Rome: Accademia Nazionale dei Lincei, 1965.

Adams, John. *The Works of John Adams.* Boston: Little, Brown, 1856.

Allier, Raoul. *Voltaire et l'affaire Calas.* Paris: Stock, 1898.

Anchel, Robert. *Crimes et châtiments au XVIIIe siècle.* Paris: Perrin, 1933.

Argental, Raoul d'. *Histoire complète de la vie de Voltaire.* Paris: Sandoz et Fischbacher, 1878.

Avray, Maurice d'. *Le Procès du chevalier de La Barre; un crime judiciare et une erreur d'opinion, d'après les documents authentiques.* Paris: Société du livre d'art, 1908.

Bar, Carl Ludwig von. *A History of Continental Criminal Law.* Boston: Little, Brown, 1916.

Barr, Mary-Margaret H. *A Bibliography of Writings on Voltaire.* New York: Institute of French Studies, 1929.

Bastard d'Estang, Henri de. *Les Parlements de France.* Paris: Didier, 1857.

Beaumont, Elie de. *Mémoire à consulter et consultation pour la Dame Anne Rose Cabibel veuve Calas et ses enfants.* Paris: Le Breton, 1762.
_____. *Mémoire à consulter et consultation pour Pierre Paul Sirven.* Paris: Cellot, 1767.

Beccaria, Cesare. *On Crimes and Punishments.* Translated with an introduction by Henry Paolucci. Indianapolis: Bobbs-Merrill, 1963.
_____. *"Des délits et des peines," traduit de l'italien par J.A.S. Collin de Plancy.* Paris: Collin de Plancy, 1823.
_____. *Dei delitti e delle pene.* 2d ed. Edited with an introduction by Piero Calamandrei. Florence: Le Monnier, 1950.
_____. *"Dei delitti e delle pene," con una raccolta di lettere e documenti relativi alla nascita dell'opera e alla sua fortuna nell'Europa del Settecento.* Edited by Franco Venturi. Turin: Einaudi, 1965.
_____. *Opere.* Edited by Sergio Romagnoli. 2 vols. Florence: Sansoni, 1958.
_____. *Opere diverse.* Edited with an introduction by Giovanni Gravier. 3 vols. Naples, 1770.
_____. *Opere scelte.* Edited with an introduction and notes by R. Mondolfo. Bologna: Cappelli, 1925.
_____. *"Traité des délits et des peines," traduit par André Morellet.* Edited by Roederer. Paris: Imprimerie du Journal de l'économie publique, de morale et de politique, 1797.
_____. *See also* Farrer, James Anson; Firpo, Luigi; Landry, Eugenio; Manzoni, Alessandro; Villari, Pasquale.

Bédarida, Henri, and Hazard, Paul. *L'Influence française en Italie au dix-huitième siècle.* Paris: "Les Belles Lettres," 1934.

Belin, J.P. *Le Mouvement philosophique de 1748 à 1789.* Paris: Belin Frères, 1913.

Bengesco, Georges. *Voltaire—Bibliographie de ses oeuvres.* 4 vols. Paris: Perrin, 1885.

Bentham, Jeremy. *A Bentham Reader*. Edited by Mary Peter Mack. New York: Pegasus, 1969.

————. *A Comment on the Commentaries—A Criticism of William Blackstone's Commentaries on the Laws of England*. Introduction and notes by Charles Warren Everett. Oxford: Clarendon Press, 1928.

————. *The Correspondence of Jeremy Bentham*. Edited by T.L.S. Sprigge. 2 vols. London: The Athlone Press of the University of London, 1968.

————. *An Introduction to the Principles of Morals and Legislation*. 1789. Edited by J.H. Burns and H.L.A. Hart. London: The Athlone Press of the University of London, 1970.

————. *The Works of Jeremy Bentham*. Publication supervised by John Bowring. 5 vols. Edinburgh: William Tait, 1843.

Berriat-Saint-Prix, Charles. *Des tribunaux et de la procédure du grand criminel au XVIIIe siècle jusqu'en 1789, avec des recherches sur la question ou torture*. Paris: Aubry, 1859.

Blackstone, William. *Commentaries on the Laws of England*. 1765. 4 vols. Philadelphia: Rees Welsh, 1898.

Bouvy, Eugène. *Le Comte Pietro Verri, ses idées et son temps*. Paris: Hachette, 1889.

————. *Paris et la société philosophique en 1766, d'après la correspondance d'un voyageur italien*. Paris: Leroux, 1891.

————. *Voltaire et l'Italie*. Paris: Hachette, 1898.

Bowle, John. *Politics and Opinion in the Nineteenth Century—An Historical Introduction*. London: Jonathan Cape, 1954.

Brissot de Warville, Jacques-Pierre. *Théorie des lois criminelles*. 1781. Paris: Aillaud, 1836.

Canetta, Rosalba, "Due note del Beccaria su controversie relative alla coltivazione del riso in Lombardia tra il 1790 e il 1794." *Archivio Storico Lombardo*, vol. 9. Milan: Società Storica Lombarda, 1971.

Cantù, Cesare. *Beccaria e il diritto penale*. Florence: Barbera, 1862.

Carter, A.T. *Outlines of English Legal History*. London: Butlerworth, 1899.

Casati, Carlo. *Lettere e scritti inediti di Pietro e Alessandro Verri*. 4 vols. Milan: Galli, 1879–81.

Cassirer, Ernst. *Die Philosophie der Aufklärung*. Tübingen: Mohr (Paul Siebeck), 1932.

Catherine the Great. *Documents of Catherine the Great—The Correspondence with Voltaire and the Instruction of 1767 in the English Text of 1768.* Edited by W.F. Reddaway. Cambridge: Cambridge University Press, 1931.

Cattelain, Fernand. *Etude sur l'influence de Montesquieu dans les constitutions américaines.* Besançon: Millot Frères, 1927.

Chassaigne, Marc. *Le Procès du Chevalier de La Barre.* Paris: Lecoffre, 1920.

Clark, Ramsey. *Crime in America—Observations on its Nature, Causes, Prevention and Control.* New York: Simon and Schuster, 1970.

Coke, Sir Edward. *The Third Part of the Institutes of the Laws of England: Concerning High Treason, and Other Pleas of the Crown, and Criminal Causes.* London: W. Clarke and Sons, 1809.

Coquerel, Athanase, fils. *Jean Calas et sa famille.* Paris: Cherbuliez, 1858.

Corpaci, Francesco. *Ideologie e politica in Cesare Beccaria.* Milan: Giuffrè, 1965.

Courtois, Louis J. *Chronologie critique de la vie et des oeuvres de Jean-Jacques Rousseau.* Annales de la société Jean-Jacques Rousseau, vol. 15. Geneva: Jullien, 1923.

Custodi, P. *Notizie di Cesare Beccaria.* In *Scrittori classici italiani di economia politica.* Milan: Destefanis, 1804.
———. *Vita di Cesare Beccaria.* In *Elogi degli illustri Italiani.* Milan: Bettoni, 1815.

De Sanctis, F. *Teoria e storia della letteratura.* Bari: Laterza, 1926.

Desjardins, Albert. *Les Cahiers des Etats généraux en 1789 et la législation criminelle.* Paris: Pedone-Lauriel, 1883.

Desnoiresterres, Gustave. *Voltaire et la société française au XVIIIe siècle.* Paris: Didier et Cie, 1871–75.

De Stefano, Francesco. *G. R. Carli (1720–1795)—Contributo alla storia delle origini del Risorgimento italiano.* Modena: Società Tipografica Modenese, 1942.

Deutsche Kriminologische Gesellschaft—Cesare Beccaria, "Dei delitti e delle pene," Zweihundert Jahre später (1764–1964). Frankfurt am

Main: Deutsche Kriminologische Gesellschaft, Jubiläums-Festschrift, 1965.

D'Hautefort, A.C.E. *Observations sur le livre des "Délits et des peines."* Amsterdam, 1767.

Diderot, Denis. *Oeuvres complètes.* Edited by J. Assezat. Paris: Garnier, 1875–77.

Eden, William, first Baron Auckland. *Principles of Penal Law.* London: White, 1771.

Esmein, Adhémar. *Histoire de la procédure criminelle en France.* Paris: Larose et Forcel, 1882.
————. *A History of Continental Criminal Procedure with Special Reference to France* (including chapters by R. Garraud and C.J.A. Mittermaier). Boston: Little, Brown, 1913.

Farrer, James Anson. *Crimes and Punishments, Including a New Translation of Beccaria's "Dei Delitti e delle Pene."* London: Chatto and Windus, 1880.

Filangieri, Gaetano. *La scienza della legislazione.* 1780–85. Edited with an introduction by P. Villari. Florence: Le Monnier, 1864.

Firpo, Luigi. *"Dei delitti e delle pene" di Cesare Beccaria, facsimile dell'edizione originale.* Turin: UTET, 1964.

Foster, Kenelm, and Grigson, Jane. *See* Manzoni, Alessandro.

Franklin, Benjamin. *The Writings of Benjamin Franklin.* Edited by Albert Henry Smyth. New York and London: Macmillan, 1905–7.

Frederick II, King of Prussia. *Oeuvres.* Berlin: Imprimerie Royale, 1848.

Halévy, Elie. *The Growth of Philosophical Radicalism.* 2d ed. Translated by Mary Morris. London: Faber and Faber, 1949.

Heath, James. *Eighteenth Century Penal Theory.* London: Oxford University Press, 1963.

Helvétius, Claude-Adrien. *Oeuvres complètes.* Paris: P. Didot l'aîné, 1795.

Hertz, Eduard. *Voltaire und die französische Strafrechtspflege im achtzehnten Jahrhundert.* Stuttgart: Ferdinand Enke, 1887.

Hodgetts, E.A. Brayley. *The Life of Catherine the Great of Russia.* London: Methuen, 1914.

Hutcheson, Francis. *An Inquiry into the Original of Our Ideas of Beauty and Virtue, in Two Treatises. I, Concerning Beauty, Order, Harmony, Design; II, Concerning Moral Good and Evil.* 1725. London: J. Darby, 1726.

Il Caffè. *Antologia de Il Caffè (1764–1766); Rassegna di una rivista.* Edited by Ezio Colombo. Milan: Bompiani, 1945.

Il Caffè, o sia Brevi e varj discorsi già distribuiti in fogli periodici. 2d ed. Venice: Pizzolato, 1766.

Jacomella, Sergio. *Nel secondo centenario del libro "Dei delitti e delle pene," 1764–1964. L'attualità del pensiero di Cesare Beccaria, per una giustizia penale più civile e più umana.* Lugano: Cenobio, 1964.

Jefferson, Thomas. *The Commonplace Book of Thomas Jefferson, A Repertory of his Ideas on Government.* Edited with introduction and notes by Gilbert Chinard. Baltimore: The Johns Hopkins Press, 1926.
———. *The Complete Jefferson.* Edited by Saul K. Padover. New York: Duell, Sloan & Pearce, 1943.
———. *The Writings of Thomas Jefferson.* Washington, D.C.: Monticello Ed., 1904.

Jousse, Daniel. *Traité de la justice criminelle de France.* 4 vols. Paris: Debure Père, 1771.

Kant, Immanuel. *Werke.* 10 vols. Vol. 5: *Metaphysik der Sitten.* Leipzig: Modes und Baumann, 1938.

Kidder, Frederic. *History of the Boston Massacre.* Albany: Joel Munsell, 1870.

Lafayette, Marquis de. *Mémoires, correspondance et manuscrits du général Lafayette, publiés par sa famille.* Brussels: Société Belge de Librairie, 1837.

Landry, Eugenio. *Cesare Beccaria, Scritti e lettere inediti raccolti ed illustrati da Eugenio Landry.* Milan: Hoepli, 1910.

Lardizabal y Uribe, Manuel de. *Discurso sobre las penas, contrahido a las leyes criminales de España para facilitar su reforma.* Madrid: J. Ibarra, 1782.

L'Averdy, Charles-Clément-François de. *Code pénal, ou Recueil des prin-*

cipales ordonnances, édits et déclarations sur les crimes et délits. 2d ed. Paris: Desaint et Saillant, 1755.

Levin, Lawrence Meyer. *The Political Doctrine of Montesquieu's "Esprit des Lois": Its Classical Background.* New York: Institute of French Studies, 1936.

Loiseleur, Jules. *Les Crimes et les peines dans l'antiquité et dans les temps modernes, étude historique.* Paris: Hachette, 1863.

Lombroso, Cesare. *Genio e degenerazione.* 2d ed. Palermo: Remo Sandron, 1907.

Madan, Martin. *Thoughts on Executive Justice.* 1784. London: J. Dodsley, 1785.

Maestro, Marcello T. *Voltaire and Beccaria as Reformers of Criminal Law.* New York: Columbia University Press, 1942; reprinted by Octagon Books, 1972.

Malthus, Thomas Robert. *An Essay on the Principle of Population.* London: J. Johnson and T. Bensley, 1803.

Mandeville, Bernard de. *An Enquiry into the Causes of the Frequent Executions at Tyburn.* London: J. Roberts, 1725.

Manzoni, Alessandro. *The Column of Infamy, prefaced by Cesare Beccaria's "Of Crimes and Punishments."* Translated by Kenelm Foster and Jane Grigson. London: Oxford University Press, 1964.

Marat, Jean-Paul. *Plan de législation criminelle.* 1780. Paris: Rochette, 1790.

Marchi, Armando De. *Cesare Beccaria e il processo penale.* Turin: Fratelli Bocca, 1929.

Maugham, Frederic Herbert. *The Case of Jean Calas.* London: Heinemann, 1928.

Mondolfo, R. *Cesare Beccaria.* Milan: Nuova Accademia Editrice, 1960.

Montanari, Antonio. *La necessità della pena di morte nella criminal legislazione, dichiarata nei casi da usarsi, con alcune osservazioni intorno a quella dei premi.* Verona: Moroni, 1770.

Montesquieu, Charles Louis de Secondat. *De l'esprit des lois.* Paris: A. Belin, 1817.

———.*Lettres persanes*. Paris: Garnier, 1960.
———. *The Spirit of Laws*. 2 vols. London: G. Bell and Sons, 1878.

Morellet, André. *Mémoires sur le dixhuitième siècle et sur la Révolution*. Paris: Ladvocat, 1821.

Morley, John Viscount. *Voltaire*. London: Macmillan, 1923.

Muratori, Lodovico Antonio. *Le Opere*. Edited by G. Falco and F. Forti. Milan and Naples: Ricciardi, 1964.

Muyart de Vouglans, Pierre-François. *Lettre concernant la réfutation de quelques principes hasardés dans le "Traité des délits et des peines."* Paris: Desaint, 1767.
———. *Les lois criminelles de France, dans leur ordre naturel*. Paris: Barrois, 1783.

Noyes, Alfred. *Voltaire*. New York: Sheed and Ward, 1936.

Overbeck, Alfred von. *Das Strafrecht der französischen Encyclopädie*. Karlsruhe: G. Braun, 1902.

Paley, William. *Moral and Political Philosophy*. 1785. New York: S. King, 1824.

Pastoret, Claude-Emmanuel de. *Des loix pénales*. Paris: Buisson, 1790.

Pecchio, Giuseppe. *Storia dell' economia pubblica in Italia*. 1829. Turin, 1852.

Pennsylvania Statutes. *An Act for the Better Preventing of Crimes and for Abolishing the Punishment of Death in Certain Cases*. Philadelphia: T. Bradford, 1794.

Philippon de La Madelaine, Louis. *Discours sur la nécéssité et les moyens de supprimer les peines capitales*. Paris, 1770.

Phillipson, Coleman. *Three Criminal Law Reformers: Beccaria, Bentham, Romilly*. London: J.M. Dent and Sons, 1923.

Pike, Luke Owen. *A History of Crime in England*. 2 vols. London: Smith, Elder, 1873–76.

Poore, Perley. *The Federal and State Constitutions, Colonial Charters and Other Organic Laws of the United States*. 2d ed. Washington, D.C.: Government Printing Office, 1878.

Radzinowicz, Leon. *A History of English Criminal Law and its Administration from 1750—The Movement for Reform 1750–1833.* New York: Macmillan, 1948.

Rambaud, Alfred. *Histoire de la Russie depuis les origines jusqu'à nos jours.* 6th ed. Paris: Hachette, 1914.

Renazzi, Filippo Maria. *Elementa juris criminalis.* 1773–81. 3 vols. Rome: Poggioli, 1802.

Riformatori lombardi, piemontesi e toscani. Edited by Franco Venturi. Vol. 3 of *Illuministi Italiani.* Milan and Naples: Ricciardi, 1958.

Riformatori napoletani. Edited by Franco Venturi. Vol. 5 of *Illuministi Italiani.* Milan and Naples: Ricciardi, 1962.

Risi, Paolo. *Animadversiones ad criminalem jurisprudentiam pertinentes.* Milan: Galeazzi, 1766.

Robespierre, Maximilien. *Oeuvres complètes.* Paris: Leroux, 1910.

Romilly, Sir Samuel. *Observations on the Criminal Law of England, as it Relates to Capital Punishments, and on the Mode in Which it is Administered.* London: T. Cadell, 1810.

Rousseau, Jean-Jacques. *Oeuvres complètes.* Paris: Furne et Cie, 1889.

Rusca, Franchino. *Osservazioni pratiche sopra la tortura.* Lugano, 1776.

Rush, Benjamin, M.D. *Considerations of the Injustice and Impolicy of Punishing Murder by Death.* Philadelphia: Mathew Carey, 1792.

Sarton, George. "Beccaria (1738–94)." *Bulletin of the History of Medicine.* Supplement no. 3. Baltimore: Johns Hopkins University Press, 1944.

Scaduto, Francesco. *Cesare Beccaria.* Palermo: Remo Sandron, 1913.

Seregni, Giovanni. *Dal Carteggio di Pietro e Alessandro Verri—Lettere edite e inedite.* Milan: Leonardo, 1943.

Servan, Antoine Joseph Michel. *Discours sur l'administration de la justice criminelle.* Geneva, 1767.

Smith, Adam. *An Inquiry into the Nature and Causes of the Wealth of Nations.* London: W. Strahan and T. Cadell, 1776.

Sonnenfels, Joseph von. *Su l'abolizione della tortura (Ueber die Abschaffung der Tortur*, 1775). Milan: Galeazzi, 1776.

Spirito, Ugo. *Da Beccaria a Carrara. Storia del diritto penale italiano*, vol. 1. Rome: De Alberti, 1925.

Spurlin, Paul Merrill. *Montesquieu in America 1760–1801*. Baton Rouge: Louisiana State University Press, 1940.

Stephen, James Fitzjames. *A History of the Criminal Law of England*. 3 vols. London: Macmillan, 1883.

Torrey, Norman L. *The Spirit of Voltaire*. New York: Columbia University Press, 1938.

Turnbull, Robert J. *A Visit to the Philadelphia Prison, containing an Account of the Gradual Reformation and Present Improved State of the Penal Laws of Pennsylvania, with Observations on the Impolicy and Injustice of Capital Punishment*. Philadelphia: 1796; reprinted by James Phillips & Son (London), 1797.

Van Doren, Carl. *Benjamin Franklin*. New York: Viking Press, 1938.

Venturi, Franco, *Settecento riformatore—Da Muratori a Beccaria*. Turin: Einaudi, 1969.

Verri, Pietro. *Carteggio di Pietro e di Alessandro Verri dal 1766 al 1797*. Vols. 1–6, Milan: Cogliati, 1910–28; vols. 7–9, Milan: R. Deputazione di storia patria per la Lombardia, 1931–37; vols. 10–12, Milan: Giuffrè (under the auspices of R. Deputazione di storia patria per la Lombardia), 1939–42. Publication discontinued in 1942 after vol. 12, which contains letters up to September 1782.
_____. *Osservazioni sulla tortura*. In *Scrittori classici italiani di economia politica*. Milan: Destefanis, 1804.
_____. *Scritti vari*. 2 vols. Florence: Le Monnier, 1854.

Vianello, C.A. *La vita e l'opera di Cesare Beccaria, con scritti e documenti inediti*. Milan: Ceschina, 1938.
_____. *Le consulte amministrative inedite di Cesare Beccaria*. Milan: Giuffrè, 1943.

Villa, C.P. *Notizie intorno alla vita ed agli scritti del Marchese Cesare Beccaria Bonesana*. In *Opere di Cesare Beccaria*. 2 vols. Milan: Società tipografica dei Classici Italiani, 1821–22.

Villari, Pasquale. *Discorso sulla vita e le opere dell'autore*. In *Le Opere di Cesare Beccaria*. Florence: Le Monnier, 1854.

Visconti, A. *Le Scuole Palatine di Milano*. Milan: L. Bonfiglio, 1927.

Voltaire, François-Marie Arouet. *Oeuvres complètes*. Edited by L. Moland. 52 vols. Paris: Garnier, 1877–85.

Voltaire. *The Works of M. de Voltaire*. 35 vols. London: J. Newberry, 1761–65.

Zarone, Giuseppe. *Etica e politica nell' utilitarismo di Cesare Beccaria*. Naples: Istituto Italiano per gli Studi Storici, 1971.